The Classical Gardens of Suzhou

苏州古典园林

New World Press
China Translation & Publishing Corporation

World Heritage Sites in China

Chief Editors: Feng Chaoxiong, Fan Yiguang

President of New World Press: Yang Yuqian
President of China Translation & Publishing Corporation: Wu Xizeng

First Edition 2007
The Classical Gardens of Suzhou

ISBN-978-7-80228-508-8
Published and Distributed by New World Press & China Translation And Publishing Corporation

New World Press:
24 Baiwanzhuang Road, Beijing 100037, China
Website : www.nwp.cn
www.newword-press.com

China Translation And Publishing Corporation:
Floor 6 Wuhua Building, 4(A)Chegongzhuang Street, West District , Beijing 100044, China
Website: www.ctpc.com.cn

Printed in the People's Republic of China

Sponsors
Feng Chaoxiong, Jia Yanli, Zhang Hai'ou

Advisors
Shao Hua, Zhou Ganzhi, Zheng Xiaoxie, Feng Qiyong, Luo Zhewen, Meng Zhaozhen

Chief Editors
Feng Chaoxiong, Fan Yiguang

Committee Members
Zhang Hai'ou, Zhang Gaoli, Cen Hong, Luo Pingfeng, Du Li, Huang Jundu, Yao Yanxiang, Yi Xueling, Gao Zhigang, Fang Peihe, Mao Xiaowei, Yang Hui, Zhan Yongwei, Huang Wei, Zhou Qin, Jin Xuezhi, Ju Feng, Gong Kemin, Li Zhexiang, Zhao Qi, Chen Jianguo, Lu Haiyang, Xiang Huaming, Lu Caiping, Zhou Jiansheng, Zhou Jianzhong, Jiang Fanggen, Chen Zhong, Sun Zhiqin, Shen Yulin, Gao Yungen, Liu Jinde, Liu Zhiping, Feng Chaogang, Zhang Jian, Wu Zhen, Cui Jinyu, Bu Fuming, Xue Liang, Li Fusheng, Liu Qin, Zuo Ying, Zhou Juying, Wu Xiaonan, Zhou Jukun

Photographers
Shao Hua, Zhou Ganzhi, Ju Feng, Fan Yiguang, Zheng Kejun, Feng Chaoxiong, Miao Liqun, Zhou Jukun

Organizer
Suzhou Celebrity Studies Institute

World Heritage ·

China

This is a series of books about the contents and grace of the World Heritage sites in China. It is also a splendid chapter that records the remarkable achievements made by China in cooperation with the rest of the world in advocating world peace, seeking long-term benefit for mankind and protecting the common homeland of human beings around the world.

In China today, World Heritage protection has become an enlarged and deepened concept of environmental protection. Taking World Heritage protection as an integral component of the sustainable development of human society has become a public consensus. As the top-rated group of the targets placed under heritage protection, World Heritage sites in particular have won the universal care and affection of all people, with their high universal values, their scientific and strict protection concepts and mechanisms, and their fine state of conservation and management. Meanwhile, World Heritage protection has played unique, noticeable roles in improving the people's livelihood, building a harmonious society, protecting the heritage sites and environmental landscapes, and providing the best examples for modeling.

China is a country with a vast territory, numerous ethnic groups, along history and colorful cultures. The natural environment of all shapes and forms and the cultural traditions of profound meanings constitute a rich World Heritage resource. The 10-year Cultural Revolution prevented China from becoming the earliest member of the Convention concerning the Protection of World Cultural and Natural Heritages that came into force in 1972. But since the country signed the convention in 1985, World Heritage has made great progress in China. Of all the 830 sites that have been included on the World Heritage List, China claims 33, comprising 24 cultural sites, 5 natural sites and 4 mixed sites. While these sites have greatly enriched the World Heritage treasure-house and made outstanding contributions to worldwide heritage protection, environmental protection and sustainable social development, they have also promoted the understanding, friendship, cooperation and common prosperity between the Chinese people and the people in the rest of the world. In addition, they have truly stimulated the love of homeland, the sense of pride, the self-confidence and the creativeness of the people at the heritage sites. They have also promoted social harmony and progress, spurred homeland beautification, deepened conservation concepts, and improved protection techniques and management expertise.

World Heritage's work in China has demonstrated all the latest progress in this field. For example, the deepening understanding of World Heritage's emphasis on sites' universal values, authenticity, completeness and state of protection and management, the exploration and improvement of sites equilibrium and representativeness, the advocacy and respect for cultural diversity, and the continuous exploration and expansion of site varieties can all find expression in World Heritage's efforts in China.

While the cause of world heritages develops, the publicity and demonstration of these heritages should also continue to develop. The World Heritage • China series, which now sets its sail, will not only cover the 33 heritage sites already included on the List by 2006, but also bring in one new beautiful face after another. Along with the existing sites, the new comers with unique images and contents and representing different ethnic groups and regions will further enrich the heritage treasure-house of the Global Village. Cultural sites, industrial sites, scientific sites and agricultural sites will appear one after another. The world heritages in China will make greater contributions to the cooperation and development between the people of various countries and to the harmonious coexistence between man and nature. Presenting them to the whole world in a continuous, timely, vivid and truthful manner and making them available for the common admiration, love and enjoyment of human society has apparently become a glorious mission for the series of books.

Guo Zhan
ICOMOS Vice President
ICOMOS/China Vice President & Secretary-General

Beijing, September 6, 2006

Preface

It is universally acknowledged that the time-honored classical gardens of China serve as an exquisite showcase of unique styles and superb techniques of garden construction. Jellicoe, the late garden expert, once commented that Chinese gardens rank at the top of all of the world's gardens, and that it is impossible to talk about gardens without mentioning China.

As a matter of fact, the culture of Chinese classical gardens has two main aspects: one is the gardens themselves; the other is the literature concerning them. Although there are not many gardens that have been preserved perfectly down through the ages, we still have quite a few garden-related relics and documents, the study of which forms a brilliant part of our cultural heritage in its own right.

The earliest instances of garden parks in China can be traced back to the Yin and Shang dynasties (around 1,000 BC). Three Chinese characters, 囿，苑，圃 (*you, yuan, pu*), all of which mean "garden", can be found carved on tortoise shells from those periods. "*You*" was a type of royal garden where birds and beasts were kept, while "*pu*" was a garden exclusively for plants. In the Qin Dynasty (221- 206 BC), "*you*" became "*yuan*". Later, in the Han Dynasty (206 BC- AD220), gardens with edifices could be found on royal grounds. Artistic development during the Wei and Jin period (220- 420), as seen mainly in the realms of poetry and painting, paved the way for the art of garden construction. In the Sui and Tang period (581- 907), economic prosperity allowed for the large-scale construction of private gardens all around major cities and their suburbs. Regrettably, none of these private gardens remain today. Gardens are different from other constructions in that they can't be preserved without any change. Thus, only through the combination of relics and documents can we learn about how they once appeared. The oldest gardens that still exist today are probably in Shanxi, Sichuan and Hangzhou. They date back to the late Tang Dynasty.

History saw many changes as dynasties rose and fell. One thing that didn't change, however, was the Chinese predilection to build gardens that reflect nature. From the Tang and Song dynasties (600- 900) and on through the centuries, gardens were designed to replicate nature in miniature. Garden making throve from the 9th century until the 12th century, as is attested to by many contemporary literary records.

According to the findings of Wang Jüyuan, it was between the 9th and 13th centuries that Chinese landscape garden design reached its maturity. Landlords, officials, scholars and men of letters all indulged themselves in the prosperity of city life, but they also longed for some sort of harmony with nature. These were the men who built private gardens. The gardens were constructed in confined areas, but by dint of their ingenious, artistic arrangements they were able to satisfy the aesthetic demands of their owners. We know of these gardens today through a large corpus of landscape paintings and scholastic poetry.

After the Song and Yuan periods, Chinese classical garden design developed further, and reached a new peak of maturity in the Ming and Qing dynasties (1368- 1911). During this period of development, countless talented artisans devoted themselves to the craft of gardens, and a bulk of literature concerning the theoretical aspects of garden design was written. *Craftsmanship of Garden Design*, written by Ji Cheng in the Ming Dynasty, is a very good example. Many classical gardens from this period can still be seen today. Generally, such gardens are divided into two categories, i.e. imperial gardens and private gardens. The former are mainly located in Beijing, and the latter can be found throughout the Yangtze delta, most notably in Suzhou.

There are sound reasons, historically, for Suzhou's gardens to be regarded as China's finest. The earliest garden in Suzhou, which belonged to the King of Wu, was built 2,500 years ago. The Surging Waves Pavilion, which was built in the 11th century, is one of the best examples of the philosophy of "man-made yet natural" that is so prevalent in the construction of Chinese garden edifices. There were over 270 gardens in Suzhou during the Ming Dynasty, and the total number reached about 300 during the Qing Dynasty. When the People's Republic of China was founded in 1949, there were about a hundred gardens left, 70 of which have survived down to the present. They are all meticulously maintained, and nine of them are listed as UNESCO World Heritage sites.

During the Ming and Qing periods, the design of some gardens was heavily influenced by the art of painting. Gardens were laid out not only to imitate natural scenery, but also to satisfy their owners' intellectual and emotional tastes. A case in point is the Lion Forest Garden, constructed by monks in the 14th century. Its grotesque rockery does not seek to replicate nature; rather, it is a group of abstract lion sculptures. This also holds true for the Humble Administrator's Garden, the Lingering Garden, the Master of Nets Garden, as well as several others. We can appreciate them from many perspectives, as each of them continues to offer fresh visual satisfaction.

It is hard to generalize about the merits of the gardens of Suzhou. They are a magnificent part of our cultural heritage; they are a crystallization of human wisdom. Many details of ancient garden design are yet to be discovered. However, I think it is safe to say that the gardens of Suzhou all have the following four features:

First, the gardens of Suzhou all seek to imitate nature, and to augment that imitation with artificial elements. The philosophical basis for this predilection is deeply rooted in traditional Chinese culture. Gardens are arranged to project a so-called "man-made yet natural" aura. This cannot be fulfilled solely through the arrangement of a landscape – the garden designer's own aesthetic views also play an equally important role. Chinese classical gardens are a perfect integration of nature and work by man. They are an imitation of nature, and fully manifest the beauty of nature. They can also be seen as an improvement on nature, one from which the light of human artistic genius shines.

Second, though there are some general patterns that were observed in most of Suzhou's gardens, each garden still maintains its own unique, exquisite design. Rules do exist and there are a few uniform styles, but there are still numerous possibilities for variation. Furthermore, we can't get a true sense of one of these gardens simply by looking at pictures. They are organized too compactly. Ji Cheng described such compactness in his book *The Craftsmanship of Garden Building*, in a passage that details the ten elements of garden design.

Third, each garden is an all-encompassing piece of art. Having the same aesthetic elements found in architecture, poetry, calligraphy and painting, those pictures, steles, plaques and door-side inscriptions found in the gardens not only serve to enhance the beauty of the grounds, but also contain extensive cultural connotations.

Fourth, there are general rules, but no fixed laws in garden making. Classical gardens with their distinctive styles may seem to have ossified somewhere, but as people pursued the mastery of garden art, building techniques were developed and perfected, lending a uniqueness to each and every specimen. The close relationship between architecture and environment is arguably the most notable element of classical garden design. A wonderful example of the sophistication of this relationship can be seen at Canli Garden in Suzhou. Small as it is, measuring only 140 square meters, it still projects an extremely pictorial and poetic mood.

The classical gardens of Suzhou contain much for us to explore. It is truly a pity that so few of them are still around. The ones that remain are treasures indeed.

In conclusion, I would like to emphasize that maintenance is the work of many generations. It will be our children's responsibility to care for and rejuvenate the cultural treasures of China. I sincerely hope that the publication of this book will contribute to the protection, research and development of China's cultural treasures.

Beijing, 2007

— Zhou Ganzhi, President of the Chinese Society of Landscape Architecture, Academician at the Chinese Academy of Science and the Chinese Academy of Engineering

Bei jing
Jiang su
Su zhou
Nanjing
Suzhou

World Heritage Sites in China

The Classical Gardens of **Suzhou**

Chief Editors: Feng Chaoxiong, Fan Yiguang

The cultural heritage of the classical gardens of Suzhou is appreciated all over the world.

Congratulations on the publication of *The Classical Gardens of Suzhou*

One

White walls enclose quietness
within the busy town,
And garden life of bounty in the
fairyland.
The rockery peaks, ranges and
streams contain much;
All old-style buildings far from
the world noises stand.
As every plant and flower plays
with its shadow,
The seasons change, without
extremes at either end.
Out of broken silence sound the
tunes of pipe's string,
Finding all over the world fans if
not a band.

Two

As all arts are valued in both form
and substance,
Suzhou's best scenes are in her
classical gardens.
Made as if by Nature's hand
in smaller size,
They find roots in the nation's
spiritual essence.

鄭孝燮

——Zheng Xiaoxie, Vice Chair of the Expert Committee on National Historic and Cultural Cities Protection

蘇州園林
江南獨秀
丁亥正月
謝辰生

Suzhou Gardens, unique flowers of the Yangtze delta
January 2007

——Xie Chensheng, Advisor of the National Relics Authority

Appreciating classical gardens Savoring the arts

——Congratulations on the publication of your picture book, *The Classical Gardens of Suzhou.*

Mid-Spring, 2007

——Feng Qiyong, Former Vice President of the China Arts Academy, President of the China National Study Academy (Guoxue Academy)

世界遗产苏州园林

题辞

苏州以其得天独厚的山川湖泊自然条件和悠久的历史文化传统，加之能工巧匠们的创造智慧，造就了许多精美绝伦的园林，荣获了"苏州园林甲天下"和"人间天堂"的称号。苏州古典园林以其高度的历史艺术价值被列为了全国重点文物保护单位和世界遗产的名录。半个多世纪以来，我曾多次来到苏州为苏州园林之保护维修及遗产之申报进行考察研究。深受苏州园林之感染与熏陶，曾写小词之赞之。今恭书二首以为此书出版之祝贺

一、望江南　苏州园林

姑苏好，天下甲园林。叠石漏窗频换景，亭廊池榭逐幽深，花树四时春。

二、虞美人　馆娃宫怀古

灵岩山寺青青草，细雨流光照。吴山隐约下余晴。烟树迷离人散，渐黄昏。馆娃宫殿今何在，遗址几更改。年年岁岁旧情思，响屧廊声躧向有谁知。

注：馆娃宫为两千多年前苏州之名园。全国最早的帝王宫苑之一。

丁亥之春

罗哲文并书

China's World Heritage: The Classical Gardens of Suzhou

Suzhou is in the enviable position of having beautiful lakes and streams, a long history and a profound cultural tradition, along with the cumulative wisdom of many professional masters of construction. All these factors contribute to the unparalleled beauty of Suzhou's gardens. This is why people say that Suzhou is paradise on Earth. With their immeasurable historic and artistic value, the classical gardens of Suzhou are protected by the national government and have a place on UNESCO's list World Cultural Heritage sites. I myself often make trips to Suzhou's magnificent gardens in a professional capacity. They have left a deep impression on me. Allow me to celebrate the publication of this book with two poems:

One
Suzhou is beautiful,
Its gardens are the world's best.
Their tall rockeries and elegant windows
make kaleidoscope scenes:
Pavilions, corridors and verandas
deep in the woods of evergreen plants
and flowers.

Two
Around Lingyan Mountain Temple the grass is green;
Time passes through streaming sunlight and drizzling rain,
That blurs the Wu's Mount when the day is to clear up again.
Cloudy woods look fuzzy, and people live far away,
The day draws to evening.
The ancient Guanwa Palace is now lost,
And its traces never the same all times.
But all times, the beauty is not forgot,
With her wood-sole shoes' steps still echoing about.

*Guanwa Palace, built two millennia ago, was one of the earliest royal palaces, and had a famous garden.

Spring, 2007

——Luo Zhewen, Director of the National Relics Authority, Vice Chair of the Expert Committee on National Historic and Cultural Cities Protection

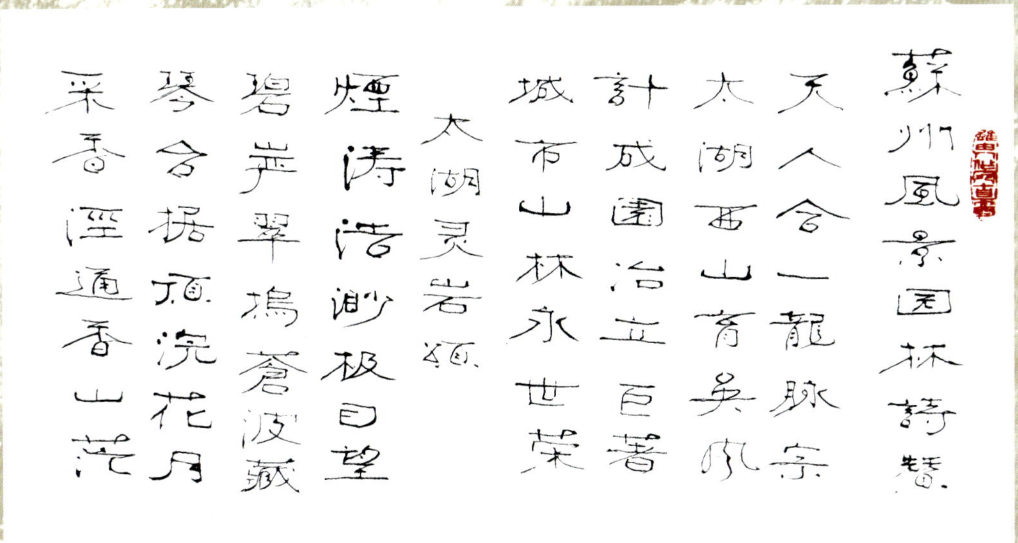

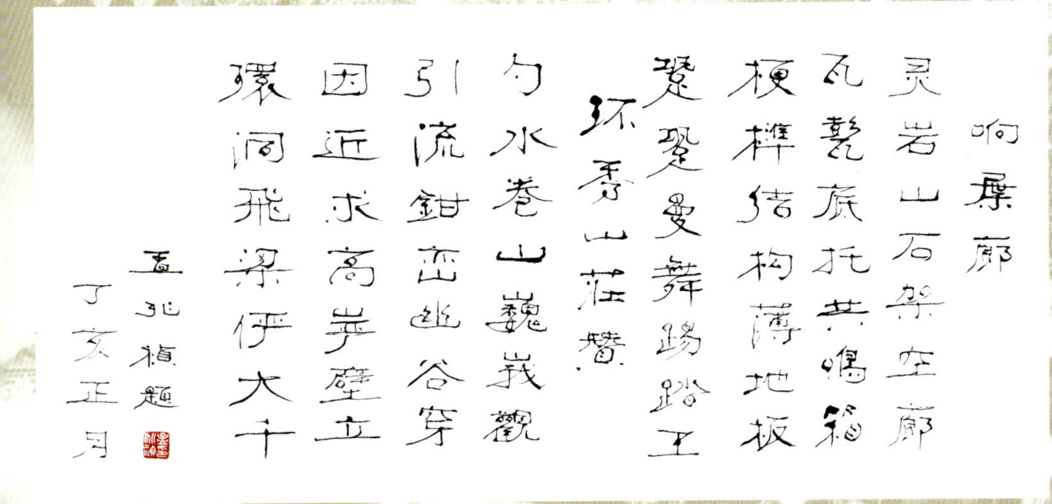

In Praise of the Scenic Gardens of Suzhou

Like a dragon, Nature and Man as one,
Hills and lakes in the style of Wu;
Gardens arranged, the masterpiece done,
The city is given the honor it's due.

Song of Lingyan and Lake Tai

A misty view of a shrouded lake,
A hint of hidden hills;
A stage where moonlit blossoms quake,
Where mountain fragrance dwells.

Corridor of Resounding Wooden Sandals

Mount Lingyan has a passage that goes over rocks,
And earthen jars, too, that are a sound box;
When on the passage's light wooden boards,
Trod dancers – music for kings and for lords!

The Mountain Villa with Embracing Beauty

A miniature landscape of hills and streams
Offsets the fearsome cliffs nearby;
And labyrinth caves like small church naves
Reach with rocky fingers towards the sky.

January 2007

——Meng Zhaozhen, Academician at the Chinese Academy of Engineering, Vice Chairman of the Chinese Society of Landscape Architecture

Classical Chinese garden design, which seeks to recreate natural landscapes in miniature, is nowhere better illustrated than in the four gardens in the historic city of Suzhou. They are universally acknowledged to be masterpieces of the genre. Dating from the 16th-18th centuries, they reflect in their meticulous design the profound metaphysical importance of natural beauty in Chinese culture.

——Cited from records of the 21st conference of the UNESCO World Heritage Committee

In spite of the endless changes in the layout of the Chinese garden (written as 園 or simplified as 园), it nevertheless can be understood as contained in the shape of "園". And the illustration is: "口" refers to the enclosing wall; "土" is similar in shape to the roof structure and may also represent the pavilion. "口" is placed in the center and thus may also be a pool; "𧘇" stands in the front as a pomegranate tree.

——Cited from Records of Jiangnan Gardens, by Tong Jun

Contents

I – An Overview of the Classical Gardens of Suzhou

As a famous old saying goes, "The gardens of Jiangnan, south of the Yangtze, are the finest on earth, and the gardens of Suzhou are the finest in Jiangnan." Suzhou has been one of the cultural and economic centers of China since the Spring and Autumn Period. It lies in an auspicious position and has abundant natural produce. Over the years, many talented people have called Suzhou home. Over the period of the Six Dynasties, through the Tang, Song, Yuan, Ming and Qing dynasties, garden construction developed rapidly in the city. Its classical gardens took a unique position in the history of garden construction. With a history of 2,500-odd years, the number of gardens there grew to exceed 800, with 70 surviving to the present day. Currently 27 of these gardens are open to the public. One can seldom find so many well-preserved gardens in a single city.

Suzhou not only has the most such gardens of any city in China, but its gardens are also of the highest artistic merit. Its most representative gardens are the Humble Administrator's Garden, the Lingering Garden, the Surging Waves Pavilion, the Master of Nets Garden, the Mountain Villa with Embracing Beauty, the Lion Forest Garden, the Garden of the Couple's Retreat, the Garden of Cultivation and the Garden of Meditation.

The first instance of a garden in Suzhou, which belonged to the King of Wu, dates back to the Spring and Autumn Period. The Pijiang Garden, Suzhou's first private garden, dates back to the Jin Dynasty. After these early gardens, the art of garden making developed through three stages. The first stage featured a tendency to imitate paradise fairylands. The second stage was characterized by an aesthetic return to nature. The third stage saw people building gardens suitable not only for sightseeing, but also for dwelling. The purpose of this sort of garden was to achieve the effect of "tranquility of resigned life within the garden, despite the city's hustle and bustle outside".

These gardens' unique charm led to their entry on the role of World Cultural Heritage sites. So far, nine gardens in Suzhou have been thusly honored. People from home and abroad all flock to see Suzhou's glamorous gardens. They function as a showcase of Chinese culture to the world.

1. The Gardens of Suzhou in History

In the course of over 2,500 years' history, an abundance of classical sites has developed in Suzhou as a direct result of the city's tradition of garden making. These sites are shining pearls of mankind's treasure of cultural history. They are scattered throughout and about the city of Suzhou.

The history of garden making in Suzhou can be traced back to the off-residence villas of the royal family in the State of Wu in the Spring and Autumn Period. As described in the historic records, the earlier kings of Wu all had enclosed parks and gardens built outside the ancient town. Even today we can still visit the site of one of these gardens, which is named Guanwa Palace. Many gardens were built in the centuries that followed the Spring and Autumn Period. Certain gardens have come to represent the prevailing tastes of each period. From the Song and Yuan dynasties, the unique art of garden construction gradually developed its own characteristics. It reached such a height in the Ming and Qing dynasties that many of the gardens of those periods were considered to be unequalled by gardens anywhere in the whole nation. Among them there are the Humble Administrator's Garden, the Lingering Garden, the Master of Nets Garden, the Mountain Villa with Embracing Beauty, the Surging Waves Pavilion, the Lion Forest Garden, the Garden of Cultivation, the Garden of the Couple's Retreat and the Garden of Meditation. These gardens are now considered to be the best examples of Chinese classical gardens.

Collected Paintings of the Scenic Spots of Suzhou by Shen Zhou (Ming Dynasty)

Detail from an image of the Surging Waves Pavilion (stone engraving, Qing Dynasty)

Painting of the Lion Forest Garden by Ni Zan (Yuan Dynasty)

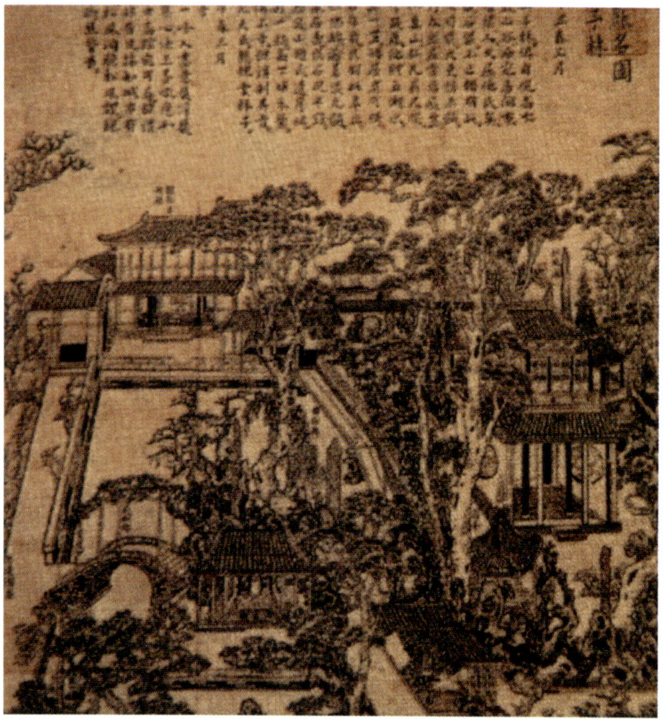

Taohuawu woodcut print of the Lion Forest Garden (Qing Dynasty)

Detail from a painting of the Twelve Limestone Peaks at Hanbi Mountain Villa by Wang Xuehao (Qing Dynasty)

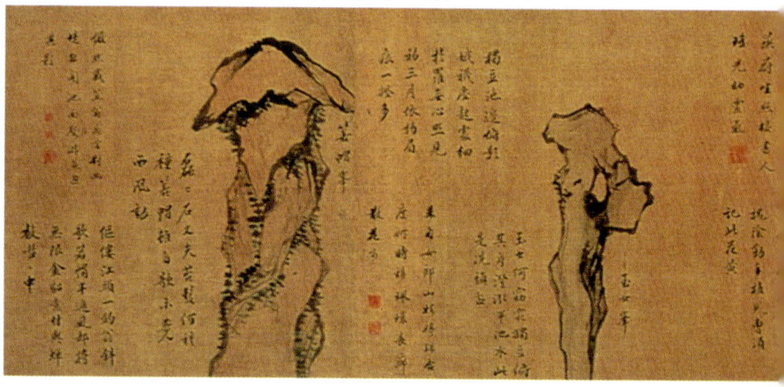

Detail from a painting of the East Garden by Wen Zhengming (Ming Dynasty)

Painting of the Humble Administrator's Garden by Wen Zhengming (Ming Dynasty)

Painting of the Humble Administrator's Garden by Wen Zhengming (Ming Dynasty)

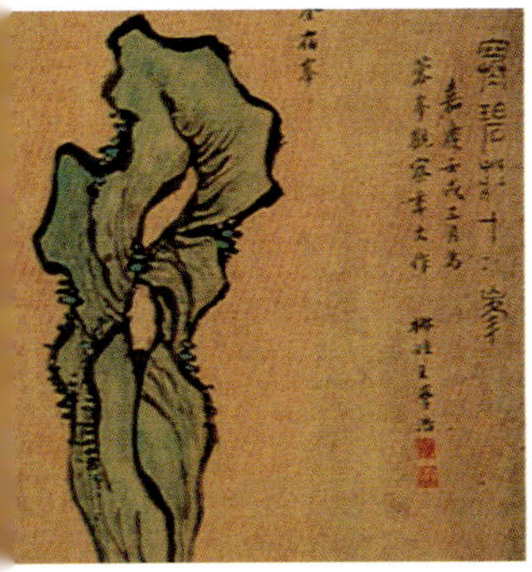

Painting of Lanxue Hall by Liu Yu (Qing Dynasty)

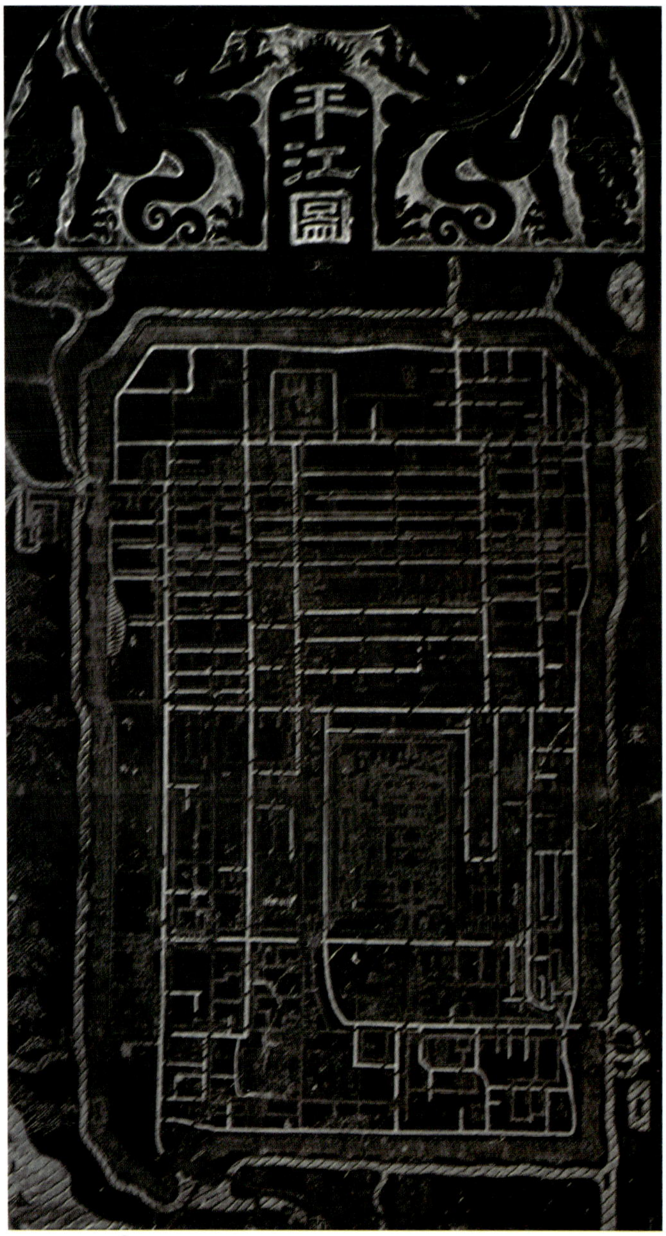

This stone engraving of a map of Pingjiang, inscribed during the Southern Song Dynasty (1127- 1279), is a dramatic record of the historical appearance of that prosperous town. It was at this time, too, that the Chinese art of landscape painting reached its zenith; the people of that era called landscape paintings "humanitarian paintings". The special illustrations embellishing this map are evidence of the importance of garden parks in this period of history.

Lingyan Mountain is situated in Suzhou's suburb of Mudu, near Lake Tai. It is about 10 kilometers west of the city. Here, atop the mountain is the site of Guanwa Palace, built over two millennia ago by the King of Wu. Mudu is well-known for its private Ming and Qing gardens.

2. Canonical Gardens

Around 70 of the 300-plus classical gardens built during the Ming and Qing dynasties are now protected sites. Twenty-seven of these are currently open to the public. First of all, let's take a look at the gardens included in UNESCO's list of World Cultural Heritage sites. The Humble Administrator's Garden has its eastern section arranged in a rustic style; its middle section emphasizes water; and the west part is notable for its winding corridors. The Lingering Garden demonstrates a compact layout. The Master of Nets Garden is in the style of a traditional Suzhou residence, which combines garden space and living space into a seamless whole. The Mountain Villa with Embracing Beauty is famous for its rockery, designed by Ge Yuliang, the master of rock arrangement. The Surging Waves Pavilion, built in a unique style, makes use of the scenery outside, as well as inside, the garden. The Lion Forest Garden, which is also known as the Rockery Kingdom, was praised by architect I.M. Pei for its natural and picturesque scenes. The Garden of Cultivation resembles a panoramic landscape painting. The outstanding feature of the Garden of the Couple's Retreat is its many references to its "couple" theme. The Garden of Meditation, with various structures around its central pond, is a unique water garden.

These are, of course, only a few of the charming gardens Suzhou has to offer. Other beautiful and, indeed, canonical gardens in the city are the Garden of Harmony, Qu Yuan Garden, He Yuan Garden (Crane Garden), Banyuan Garden (Half Garden), Listening to the Maples Garden and Huiyin Garden.

Strolling through these gardens, we can appreciate the art of garden design and get a sense of the humanitarian and poetic elements of nature.

The Humble Administrator's Garden, regarded as one of the four finest classical gardens in China, was built in the Zhengde Period (1506-1521) of the Ming Dynasty by Wang Xianchen. The garden's name refers to its verdant vegetables, which made it a suitable residence for a minor administrator after he retired from government service. This 500-year-old garden park has three parts, an eastern part, a middle part and a western part. The middle part is generally regarded to be the finest, although the other two parts are certainly not without their attractions.

The garden primarily consists of a scenic area with open patches of water, and a main pond that occupies one fifth of the garden's total area. The majority of the structures in the garden are by the water. Over ten buildings in the garden have names that make reference to lotus blossoms. This is due to the beautiful lotus flowers in the pond. Every year there is a lotus blossom festival celebrated in this garden.

A panoramic view of the Humble Administrator's Garden

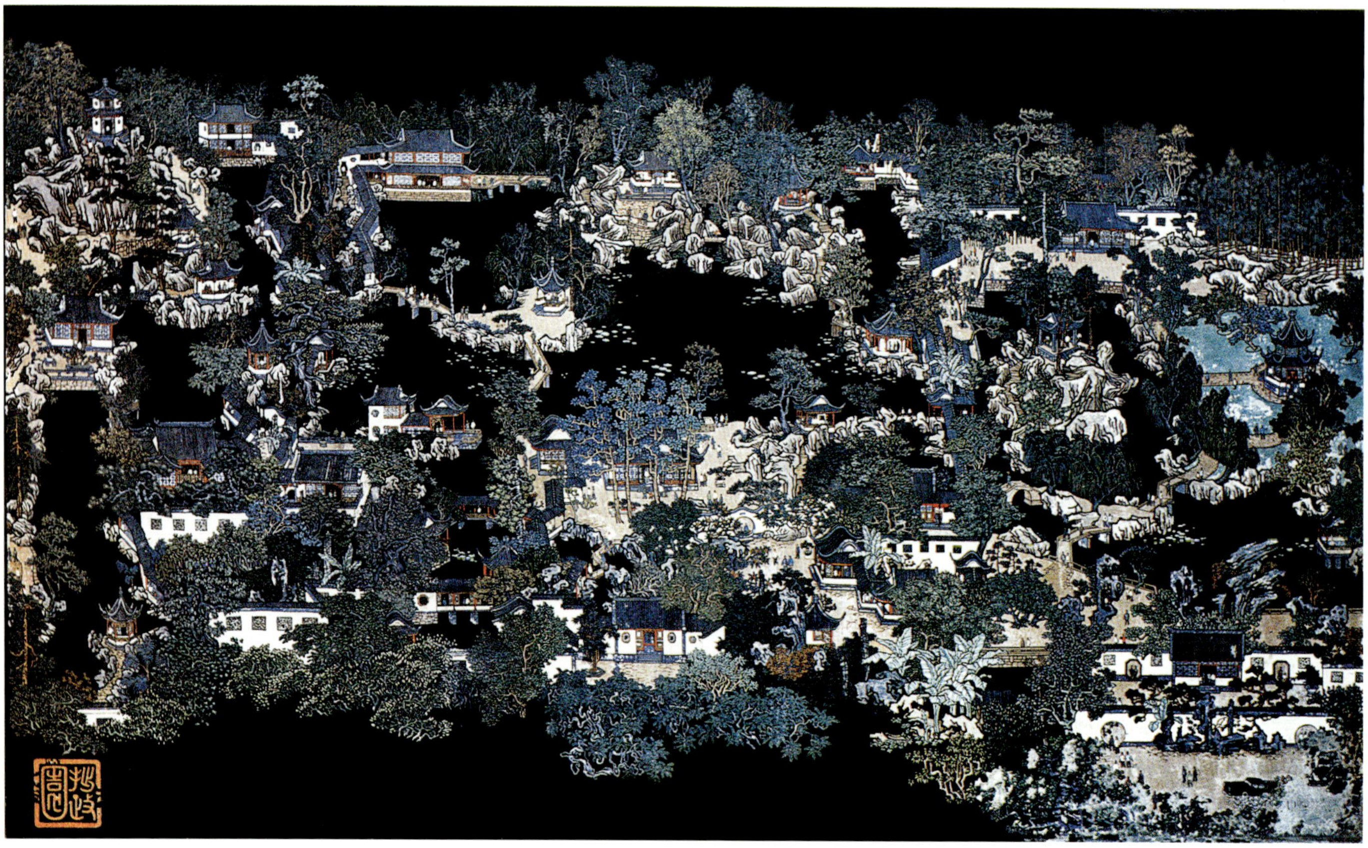

The Tower Reflection Pavilion

The Boat-like Fragrant Isle

The scenery of the eastern section

Door-side inscriptions at the Tranquil Residence Among Phoenix Trees and Bamboo

A scene in the Humble Administrator's Garden, set against the distant Beisi Pagoda

The Little Canglang

The Lingering Garden is another of China's four finest classical gardens. Built by Xu Taishi under the reign of Wanli (1573-1620) in the Ming Dynasty, it was regarded as one of the finest of Suzhou's gardens even right after its construction. During the reign of Jiaqing in the Qing Dynasty (1796- 1821), its name was changed to Hanbi Villa, and twelve signature limestone peaks were added. By the end of the reign of Tongzhi (1862- 1875), it had been renovated by Sheng Xuanhuai and his father. It was then that the garden was given its present name. The garden has three parts, namely eastern, western and middle areas. Each has its own distinctive features, but they are all highly regarded for the exquisite design and craftsmanship that they display.

A panoramic view of the Lingering Garden

Various window designs at the entrance

A roofed walkway going up the mountain

The Mingse Building

The Old Hermit Scholar's House

The Cloud-Capped Peak

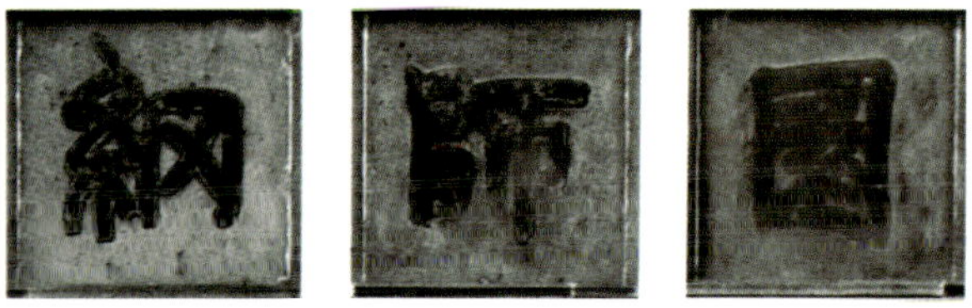

The Master of Nets Garden is an outstanding example of Suzhou's unique "mini-garden" style. In the Southern Song Dynasty, Shi Zhengzhi built the Hall of 10,000 Volumes here, with an adjacent garden called the Fisherman's Retreat. Under the reign of Qianlong (1736-1796) in the Qing Dynasty, an official named Song took it over and remodeled it. The east part of the garden features loft structures, its middle part plants and flowers, and its western part courts and halls. The combination of garden spaces and living spaces is seamless. In the early 1980's, this garden's Peony Studio was used as the model for the Ming Studio at the New York Metropolitan Museum of Art.

A panoramic view of the Master of Nets Garden

An aquatic scene at the garden

The Peony Studio

The Prune Mume Pavilion

Rockery built against the wall of the music room

Leading-to-Quietude Bridge – the garden's smallest arch bridge

The Lion Forest Garden was built as a temple estate during the Zhizheng period of the Yuan Dynasty (1342). In it there is a forest of rockery resembling a pride of lions, hence the name. According to Buddhist records, the name also makes reference to the phrase "master and disciple", since that phrase is homophonous with the word "lion" in Chinese. Emperors Kangxi and Qianlong each visited this garden several times, and it was used as a model for the construction of the Garden of Perfect Splendor in the imperial mountain resort of Chengde. This garden's most notable attraction is indeed its rockery, which is made of stones from Lake Tai. The stones' shapes are grotesque and fantastic, and not a little surprising. The rockery is divided into three parts, with 9 stone paths and 21 clefts. The architect I. M. Pei once praised it for its natural and picturesque scenes.

A panoramic view of the Lion Forest Garden

The "Rockery Kingdom"

The Stele Corridor

The Pavilion of Genuine Interest

A clover-shaped portal

A waterfall

A window

During the reign of Emperor Qingli (1041- 1049) in the Northern Song Dynasty, Su Shunqin purchased a plot of land and built a garden there. His garden is called the Surging Waves Pavilion, which is a name taken from a poem in the anthology *Songs of Chu*. In the Southern Song Dynasty, it was taken over by Han Shizhong. It underwent several renovations during the Qing Dynasty as well. The garden contains several stele inscribed in Emperor Kangxi's beautiful hand, as well as a stone-cut portrait of Wen Zhengming, a poem by Lin Zexu carved into stone and the Temple of 500 Sages. In the garden runs a double corridor whose length is punctuated by 108 windows. Carved onto the pavilion's stone pillars is a well-known couplet. It reads, "The gentle breeze and the bright moon cost not a single penny; but oh! how dear to me are the nearby water and distant hills!"

A print of a stone engraving of a map of the Surging Waves Pavilion

The Surging Waves Pavilion

The Surging Waves Pavilion with a backdrop of "borrowed" scenery

Several windows

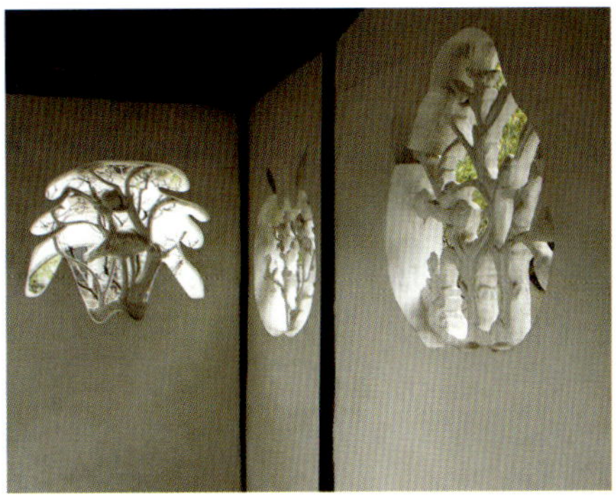

Green bamboo

A winding corridor

The Temple of 500 Sages

The Garden of Cultivation was built in the Tianqi period of the Ming Dynasty (1621- 1627) by Wen Zhengming's great grandson. Another name for this garden was the Herb Garden, for one of its owners once planted herbs in it. Its ownership changed several times. The Longevity Pavilion spans the northern edge of the pond at the center of the garden. To the south of the pond is an impressive rockery. The Ming Dynasty Fry Pavilion lies to the east of the pond. To the west is the Humble House, which served as the owner's elegant study. The general layout of the garden is centered on the pond, and the garden's main scenic spot is certainly its rockery, which lends to the landscape an extensively natural and simple look.

The Fry Pavilion

A panoramic view of the Garden of Cultivation

A portal

An aquatic scene

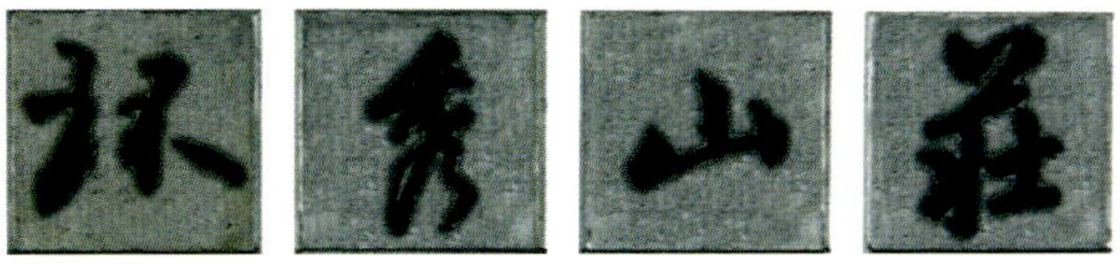

The Mountain Villa with Embracing Beauty was originally built as part of the Golden Valley Garden Park in the Song Dynasty (960- 1279). It has also gone through many hands. In the early Qing period, it was owned by Bi Yuan, and later by Ge Yuliang in the Jiaqing period (1769- 1820), under whose auspices a rockery was constructed out of huge rocks from Lake Tai. The rockery is divided into eastern and western sections, with small paths, caves, cliffs, and a stream. Today, the garden's most famous feature is still its rockery, which looks very much like real mountains in nature, with paths, caves, clefts, ravines and cliffs.

Rockery arrangement

The Asking-the-Fountain Pavilion

An ichnographic print of the Mountain Villa with Embracing Beauty

Constructed during the reign of Yongzheng (1723- 1736) in the Qing Dynasty, the Garden of the Couple's Retreat was acquired by Shen Bingcheng under the reign of Tongzhi. He went on to remodel and expand the garden. The eastern and western sections flank the garden's central residential area. In the 1930's and 1940's, educator Yang Yinyu, scholar Qian Mu and historian Gu Jiegang established a school here. The outstanding feature of the garden is its "couple" theme, as can be seen many places in both the eastern and western sections.

The great rockery design master Zhang Nanyang in the Ming Dynasty, according to professor Liu Dunzhen, arranged the garden's magnificent yellow rockery.

A woodcut gate design

Brick inscription

The Yellow Rockery

A panoramic view of the Garden of the Couple's Retreat

A government official named Ren Lansheng built the Garden of Meditation in 1885. He named it after a line from the Chinese classic *Zuozhuan*, namely “working to dedicate myself to my country, and retreating to meditate on mending my ways”. Halls, living quarters and gardens are arranged from west to east. On the second floor of one of the apartments is the famous Trotter’s Tower. With various structures around the central pond, this garden’s aquatic features are unique.

Some of the garden’s vistas were named after lines of verse written by Jiang Kui during the Southern Song Dynasty.

The Gathering Beauty Pavilion

An expanse of water

A panoramic view of the Garden of Meditation

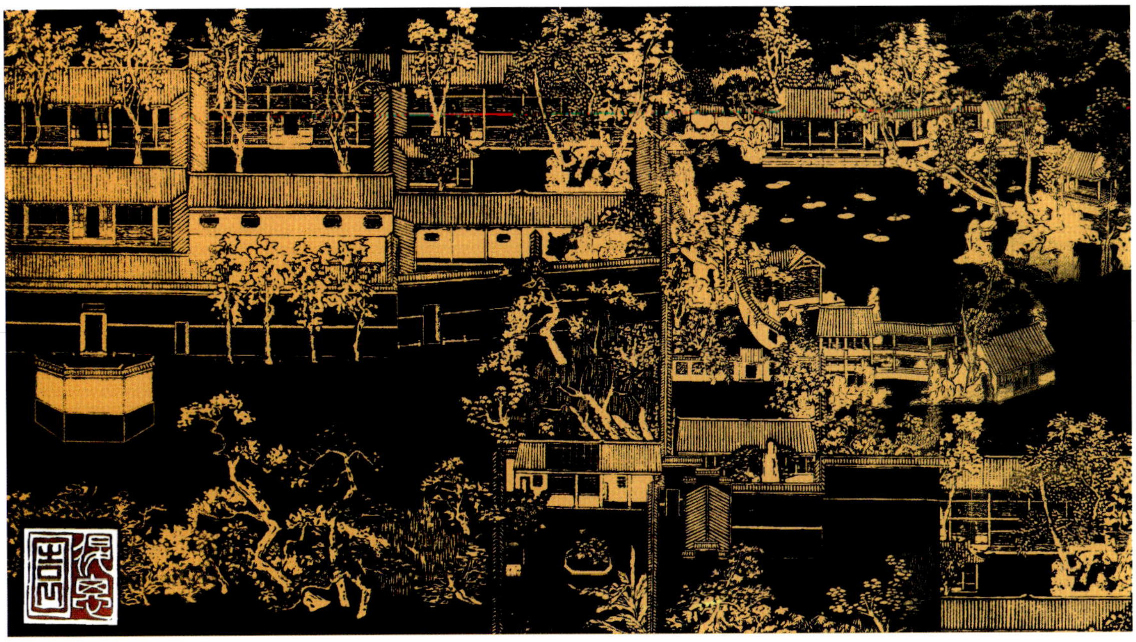

The Garden of Harmony was constructed in the Qing Dynasty. Being a small garden, situated on a plot of land measuring only 8 mu *(one mu is equal to 666.67 square meters), it was nevertheless designed and built elaborately and carefully, down to the smallest detail. The name of the garden comes from a classic literary saying; it means that a life lived harmoniously is a long and peaceful life. The names of the various structures in the garden all have literary connotations, mostly poetic ones. Almost all the most appealing elements of Suzhou garden scenery can be found here.*

Stone Conservatory in the Garden of Harmony. Its name is inscribed in the hand of a master calligrapher of the Qing Dynasty.

Yu Yue, a famous scholar of the Qing Dynasty, privately owned Quyuan Garden. The Chinese character for qu *is written as* 曲*, which also happens to resemble the garden's shape. Since the Chinese character can also be understood to mean "bending back" or "withdrawal", the name also refers to a quote from Laozi, "withdraw to safety".*

The residence in the Crane Garden is separated from the garden by a whitewashed wall that has many windows. This picture portrays the garden's winding corridor.

The Semi-Pavilion was originally built in the early years of the Qing Dynasty. The theme of being content with half can be seen in the structure of the whole garden.

The Listening -to -the -Maples Garden was originally constructed during the reign of Emperor Tiansheng (1023- 1031) of the Song Dynasty. There are ancient maple trees in the garden, hence the name. Wu Changshuo, a famous painter, once lived here and worked as painting tutor to the owner's children.

The Five Peaks Garden was built during the reign of Emperor Jiajing and was so named because of its rockery with five peaks. Here is a picture.

Huiyin Garden was first built during the Jiajing period (1522- 1567) of the Ming Dynasty and reconstructed and renamed in the 6th year of Shunzhi's reign (1650) in the Qing Dynasty. There are presently eight scenic vistas in the garden. This picture is a scene viewed from a corridor.

II – Garden Appreciation

The classical gardens of Suzhou are integrated works of art, like music: they each have their own rhythm, designed and constructed by master hands, employing extraordinary methods and techniques. The essential features of the gardens are their overall layouts, their rockery and water arrangements, construction and vegetation. By understanding these features, we can deepen our appreciation of garden design.

The overall layout represents the theme and determines the style of the garden as a whole. All the rockeries, patches of water and edifices are carefully arranged. At the center of the garden there is usually a pond that serves to frame all the surrounding scenes. These scenes contain such things as buildings, plants, corridors, pavilions, lofts and courts, which are all connected at least aesthetically, if not literally. There are endless variations on this basic design. The overall effect is that of a natural landscape.

Since rockeries and bodies of water are considered to be the soul of the garden, their arrangement and appearance are of extreme importance. Rockeries represent stasis, while aquatic elements serve to evoke a dynamic spirit. Centering on the pond, bridges and corridors link the rockery to pavilions and towers. Artistry flows through the garden along these paths. Every turn discloses a fresh view. These miniature, natural landscapes have a strong relationship with the garden designer's sense of the poetry of nature.

Buildings are also a central component of the gardens of Suzhou. It does not matter if you are a tourist or a garden owner of yesteryear – garden structures provide a spot to rest, to work, or simply to take in the view. Structures divide large swathes of garden into smaller, more manageable parts. Plants and minor buildings cluster around the main edifices, and scenes are composed through the minute arrangement of the various elements of scenery, including contrast, "borrowing", and aquatic vistas. Through the ingenious arrangement of halls, towers, pavilions, windows, walls and corridors, nature is shrunken and laid bare. The gardens of Suzhou are often compared to symphonies, in that they change and develop as you progress through them.

Vegetation is also an indispensable element of the gardens of Suzhou. Garden builders had to have an extensive knowledge of various trees and flowers. Their extensive familiarity with horticulture allowed them to carefully choose the most appropriate types of plants, determine what combination of plants to use and decide how to express a theme through vegetable arrangements. The use of plants is an extremely meaningful element of the "garden symphony".

1. Scenery and Harmony of Arrangement

When you approach a classical garden, the first thing you will notice is its layout. In line with the art of landscape painting, a garden's layout is composed of various essential elements, these being water, rockeries, structures, bridges, corridors, paths and furnishings. Generally, the very central edifices are halls, with rockeries, patches of water, and plants delicately assembled in their vicinity. All of these elements are connected by corridors and paths, and interspersed with pavilions and lofts. The interplay of these essentials is the way in which scenes are constructed. The onlooker's eyes are drawn along the garden's contours, just like admiring a picture scroll.

A deeper analysis reveals that Suzhou garden construction first emphasizes the construction of single scenic spots, which are grouped together to give the impression of an entire area or region of the garden being scenic and varied. The relationship between individual scenic spots and the scenery of an area is of great interest to the garden designer. In fact, it is in this relationship that the genius of the designer is most apparent. Though styles do vary by designer, all gardens are designed to give a consistent and developing impression from scene to scene.

The two-story Mingse Building, whose location over the water gives an impression of buoyancy.

A walkway leading to an open court

The Entrance

Laid out in a circumscribed area, entrances to Suzhou gardens are usually screened. The space is thus partitioned, and visitors are enticed to pull back the veil and view the garden's secrets. In the Lingering Garden, the entrance is located in between two buildings. Upon entry into the garden, there is a small skylight court, and only by passing through an adjacent corridor can one arrive at the Age Old Trees. On the way, one can view the middle of the garden through windows in the wall. This is a good example of the idea of "intersecting scenes".

As one travels through the maze of columns, rails and partition screens, one will travel deeper into the world of the garden. It seems there is no limit to how far the garden might extend! This technique, whose function is to increase the perceived depth of the scenery, is used to great effect in the Lingering Garden.

An alley leading from the entrance to the interior

The court in front of the Age Old Trees

A garden scene through a window in the Lingering Garden

A window in the court, through which the central garden can be seen

A scene viewed from the court in front of the Age Old Trees

The Small Huabu House as seen through an open door

A window scene from the Green Shade Pavilion

A window in a window

The middle part of the garden, as seen from the Green Shade Pavilion

Moving Through the Garden

The middle part of the Lingering Garden is organized in a ring. Moving clockwise outwards from the Green Shade Pavilion, you will first come upon the Mingse Building, from whose second floor you can look out upon a stunning aquatic vista. From there, in order, you will proceed on to the Winding Stream Tower, the West Building, the Small Fairy Isle and Haopu Pavilion; then, as you go further from here, the vista begins to narrow, focusing on smaller, elegant water arrangements; next is the Celestial Hall of the Five Peaks with its rockery; and the Cloud-Capped Pavilion on the northernmost edge of the garden. The next tour begins at the Cloud-Capped Pavilion, from where, following a counterclockwise path, you will first go to the Distant Green Loft, and then along a mosaic path and uphill through a corridor until you reach the Osmanthus Fragrance Pavilion. From the top of the rockery, there is yet another corridor which takes you to the Hanbi Mountain Villa and the Mingse Building. At this spot, there is a cave-like opening whose placard reads "Another World". Through it is the "Place of Liveliness".

The Mingse Building, situated to the west of the central scenic area

The heart of the Lingering Garden, as seen from the second floor of the Mingse Building

A map of the Lingering Garden

1. Hanbi Mountain Villa
2. The Green Shade
3. The Zigzag Stream Tower (Quxi Building)
4. The West Building
5. The Celestial Hall of the Five Peaks
6. The Peak-Worshipping Pavilion
7. The Old Hermit Scholar's House
8. The Cloud-Capped Pavilion
9. Xiyu Kuaixue Pavilion
10. Spot of Return for Reading
11. The Distant Green Loft
12. "Another" Village (You Yi Cun)
13. The Pavilion of Ultimate Pleasure
14. Shuxiao Pavilion
15. The Mingse Building at the Hanbi Mountain Villa
16. The Haopu Pavilion
17. Hall of Breeze Pond
18. Spot for Remembering the Ancients
19. Keting Pavilion
20. The Osmanthus Fragrance Pavilion

Haopu Pavilion and the Zigzag Stream Tower, seen from the Small Fairy Isle

The Mingse Building and the Hanbi Mountain Villa at dawn

A view of the West Building from the Celestial Hall of the Five Peaks

The rockery in front of the Celestial Hall of the Five Peaks

The window panels in the Celestial Hall of the Five Peaks

Looking through a window at a rockery in a courtyard

The court in front of the Cloud-Capped Tower, at the Lingering Garden's northern extremity

The Cloud-Capped Peak is a huge boulder .The Cloud-Capped Tower here creates a stylistic contrast.

Distant Green Loft

A roofed walkway leading to the Osmanthus Fragrance Pavilion

Looking up at the Osmanthus Fragrance Pavilion

"Another World". Through this door is the Place of Liveliness.

The Place of Liveliness with its winding stream. Standing in the loft by the stream, one feels as if he is straddling the water. It is a lovely place from which to watch fish.

2. Rockery and Water

Rockery and water are crucial elements of Suzhou's gardens. Garden builders sought to create miniature landscapes in which nature and architecture fuse into a coherent whole, allowing people to consider their role in nature and cultivate their temperament. Thus, rock and water arrangement is a vital element of garden design.

Rockery in Suzhou gardens fall into two main types: one is single-rock arrangement and the other is piled rocks. Stones from Lake Tai are slender, wrinkled, and pierced with holes, allowing for good drainage. Ponds in Suzhou gardens twist and turn, extending into the distance. Through rockery, still waters are brought to life. Confucius once said, "The kind find happiness in mountains, and the wise take pleasure in water." We can see the truth of this in the gardens of Suzhou.

A cliff by the water, a mountain pass through the rockery

Rockery

Rockery, in a sense, acts as the framework of gardens. In the gardens of Suzhou, most rockeries are made from limestone taken from Lake Tai, as well as other pleasing, yellowish stones. Scenes are constructed to resemble peaks, caves, cliffs, slopes, ravines – even entire mountain ranges! It is just as if these scenes were natural, if not for their scale. Sometimes a single rock can perfectly evoke an entire mountain.

Asking-the-Fountain Pavilion at the Mountain Villa with Embracing Beauty. The low, zigzagging bridge adds character to the scene while making the water seem deeper.

A cave between cliffs, with a natural stone table, stone stools and a bed

A ravine amidst peaks

Rockery at the Mountain Villa with Embracing Beauty

The rockery and the Asking-the-Fountain Pavilion at the Mountain Villa with Embracing Beauty

Two complementary peaks in the garden of the Mountain Villa with Embracing Beauty

A scene of water and rocks, as viewed from above

A view of a stone bridge from below

The yellow rockery and a path to the platform at the top of the Garden of the Couple's Retreat

An imposing rockery

Rockery in the Garden of the Couple's Retreat

The yellow rockery in the Garden of the Couple's Retreat, with its cliffs, stone steps, miniature canyons and stacked rocks, looks very much like a real mountain scene from nature. Despite its small size, it displays a great variety; each of its parts is named after its natural inspiration.

A dell between cliffs in the rockery

A view of the landscaped "Couple's Corridor" and the Mountain Water Loft as seen from the mountain top

A peak in the Lingering Garden named Yinyue, literally meaning "reflection of the moon". It is over both land and water, and it has a round hole resembling a full moon.

Rockery in the Master of Nets Garden

Rockery design in the Master of Nets Garden is made mainly from yellow granite. The granite cliff by the water resembles a wall, and hence it is known as the "Cloud Mountain Stone Wall". The rockery's surface is rough and craggy, and it very much resembles a real mountain. The section of rockery outside the "conservatory" is designed to resemble an entire mountain range.

Rockery by the conservatory wall

Rockery in the Lingering Garden

The peaks in the rockery of the Lingering Garden are mostly made from single pieces of rock from Lake Tai. This sort of construction became popular in the design of rockery gardens during the Qing Dynasty. The main peak is offset by subsidiary peaks to add to the overall effect.

The stone of the Cloud-Capped Peak, having been passed down through many hundreds of years, is the tallest of its kind in the country. Its different parts are each unique, to be sure, but this stone is more than the sum of its parts.

The yellow rockery in the Master of Nets Garden. Its appearance is quite grave, and from a distance it resembles ominous clouds, hence its other name "Cloud Mountain".

The rockery in the court of the Cloud Stairway Hall

The yellow granite rockery by the Hall of Distant Fragrance serves a double function – it screens the center of the garden from the entrance, and it also accents the hall.

Rockery in the Humble Administrator's Garden

This rockery, piled high with yellow rocks on the southern side of Distant Fragrance Hall, is truly a masterpiece. With pieces of rock irregularly arranged along the slope of the hill, it displays the true depth of the art of rock arrangement.

A rockery of earth covered with stones, with a path leading to a pavilion

The rockery of the Lion Forest Garden, based on Tianmu Mountain

Nine Lion Peak, with its million facets

Rockery in the Lion Forest Garden

The rockery in the Lion Forest garden is piled high with rocks from Lake Tai. The stones' shapes are fantastic and grotesque. In various aspects, this garden is designed to resemble Tianmu Mountain, a Buddhist retreat.

The Little Chibi, covered in yellow rocks, at the Lion Forest Garden

The mid-lake pavilion as viewed from a cave

An expanse of water in the Master of Nets Garden

Water

If a garden's bones are made of rocks, then its veins are surely made of water. In planning aquatic features in gardens, builders either made use of already-existing ponds and streams, or dug new ones. Suzhou gardens are usually centered on ponds, with radiating, meandering streams spanned by small bridges. The shores of the pond are often used in conjunction with rockery to create the impression of a cove.

Water in the Master of Nets Garden

The Master of Nets Garden is laid out around a central pond. Its yellow rockery is used as a counterpoint to its aquatic features. Some huge pieces of rock protrude over the pond, while other pieces conceal lagoons. Used in conjunction with pavilions and corridors, this deft combination of rock and water is quite striking. The All Sides Open Pavilion and the Tassel-Washing Pavilion are the garden's main scenic spots. Pleasant views can be seen from the garden's center in every direction, not to mention those views' seasonal variations.

A rivulet at the southeastern corner of the pond, made to look like the water's source

Reflection of the Tassel-Washing Pavilion

A quiet expanse of water reflecting the scenery

Across the vast expanse of water in the Garden of Meditation, one can enjoy a view of the Thatched Hut of Meditation and beyond, on to the Lotus Blooms Pavilion and the zigzagging corridor

Water in the Garden of Meditation

The Garden of Meditation is also laid out around a body of water. The main construction in this garden is the Thatched Hut of Meditation. This is a very distinctive water garden, with various structures clustered around numerous patches of water, such as the Sleeping Cloud Pavilion, the Pavilion of Rain and Cool Air and the Tower Aisle. With apartments scattered here and there, this garden truly resembles an unfurled Chinese landscape scroll. Because of the prevalence of water in its design, this garden is also called the "Water-bound Garden".

A view of the waterscape in the Garden of Meditation

A picturesque scene of rocks and water

An aquatic scene in the Garden of Cultivation

Water in the Garden of Cultivation

Here is yet another garden centered on water. There are coves at the main pond's southeast and southwest corners, spanned by low bridges. Set against the low pond are high, huge rocks with surrounding green plants, pavilions, corridors and lofts. The garden as a whole simply oozes grace and peace.

Water at the Surging Waves Pavilion

The characteristic stretches of water at the Surging Waves Pavilion rely heavily on the technique of "borrowing" scenery. A visitor can clearly see the garden's aquatic features before even entering. In this sense, water in this garden aesthetically links its exterior and interior.

Water by the Surging Waves Pavilion

A scene outside the double corridor that leads to the Facing Water Pavilion and to the Fish Viewing Spot. Reflections in the water by the banks make a vivid picture.

An expanse of water in the eastern part of the Humble Administrator's Garden

Water in the Humble Administrator's Garden

The Humble Administrator's Garden is divided into three parts — the eastern part, the middle part and the western part. They are connected mainly by water, and each has its own aquatic attractions. The eastern part has a stream that winds between banks planted with peach and willow trees. The middle part has a large lotus pond resembling a natural lake. The different styles of the structures on the water are reminiscent of dwellings along the Yangtze River.

The Little Canglang and the Small Flying Rainbow Bridge, as viewed from above

A pavilion upon the water at the Little Canglang

The Tranquil Residence among Phoenix Trees and Bamboo, seen over the pond in the Humble Administrator's Garden

The pond in the middle of the Humble Administrator's Garden at dusk reflecting the surrounding scenery

The waterfall in the western stretch of the Lion Forest Garden, its color like satin and its sound as clear as fairy music

3. Harmony in Towers, Halls, Pavilions and Corridors

The gardens of Suzhou have a great variety of exquisite structures, built with rare techniques and furnished in styles appealing to their owners' elegant, sometimes extravagant tastes. Though segmented into different areas, we may recall that garden scenes do not exist in isolation, but rather in relation to surrounding scenes and structures. Therefore buildings are indispensable to the discipline of garden design.

There are many kinds of structures in the classic gardens of Suzhou, including halls, towers, pavilions and corridors, all of which categories are subdivided according to peculiarities of function and design. Garden decorations and furnishings, including both interior and exterior items, are also an important consideration. Objects and furniture, simply put, are a part of the garden. This includes walls, wall openings, passages, portal designs, embellished window openings and walkways. Such objects are designed to work together to create a garden of beauty, as well as to express ideas that are considered auspicious in traditional Chinese culture. Some of these auspicious ideas are happiness, good luck, safety, longevity, strength and virtue.

Halls and Pavilions

Halls are the body of a garden. Relatively large in size, they are spaces for family gatherings and for entertaining guests. There are many famous halls; perhaps the most famous are the Hall of Distant Fragrance, the 36 Pairs of Mandarin Ducks Hall in the Humble Administrator's Garden, the Celestial Hall of Five Peaks, the Old Hermit Scholar's House in the Lingering Garden, the Hall of Swallow Blessing, the Flower Basket Hall in the Lion Forest Garden and the Boya Room in the Garden of Cultivation.

The Hall of Distant Fragrance in the Humble Administrator's Garden is by far the garden's most magnificent structure, with three horizontally partitioned rooms and broad windows on all sides.

The 36 Pairs of Mandarin Ducks Hall in the Humble Administrator's Garden was used by its owners for family gatherings and entertainment. Its design is unique.

The Hall of 18 Camellias, with an inscription by Lu Runxiang, a famous scholar of the Qing Dynasty

The Lixue (Standing Snow) Hall in the Lion Forest Garden, formerly used as a study. A corridor winds around three of its sides.

The Peak-Worshipping Hall in the Lion Forest Garden, facing the rockery where several ancient cypress trees gnarl the years away. The interior is furnished in Chinese redwood, and there hangs an inscribed couplet.

The Hall of Swallow's Blessing (Yanyu Hall) in the Lion Forest Garden

The Peony Studio in the Master of Nets Garden. The Chinese name of this structure literally translates to "Late Spring Studio", but peony, a flower that blooms in late spring, has become its more common appellation. This building used to serve as the owner's study. It is built in the Ming style. The couplet on the columns describes spring changing into summer.

Zaijiu (Wine-Carrying) Hall, the main hall in the Garden of the Couple's Retreat. The name is taken from a Song Dynasty poem. It refers to a secluded, content life.

The Thatched Cottage of Meditation in the Garden of Meditation. It is the garden's primary structure.

The Yiyu (Leaning on Jade) Pavilion in the Humble Administrator's Garden. It commands a broad view of the garden's various scenic spots, including the Pavilion in the Lotus Breeze.

The Prunus Mume Pavilion in the Master of Nets Garden. Walking along the veranda, one can appreciate a delightful series of views.

Towers and Pavilions on Water

Most structures termed "towers" in Suzhou gardens have two stories. Large ones are usually found in the center or along the edges of gardens, while small ones are found clustered compactly around rockeries and ponds. Lofts, on the other hand, vary in height, and often have windows on all sides. They can be found both in open areas and in hidden parts of the garden, often on top of a hill or by a pond.

The Mingse Building in the Lingering Garden, standing on the water in its unique, elegant way

The Mountain-in-View Tower to the south of the Surging Waves Pavilion

The Mountain-in-View Tower in the Humble Administrator's Garden. The name is taken from a famous line of poetry by Tao Yuanming of the Jin Dynasty. It is said to have been the office of Li Xiucheng, the royal prince of the Heavenly Kingdom in the late Qing Dynasty.

The Winding Stream Tower in the middle of the Lingering Garden. The entrance is octagonal, with the name of the tower carved into a brick placard above it.

A pavilion in the Humble Administrator's Garden, named "The Floating Green"

The Pavilion of Resting in the Clouds, an octagonal double-roofed pavilion in the Lion Forest Garden

The Gathering Beauty Pavilion, situated to the north-west of the pond, is the best spot for appreciating the garden's large-scale beauty

The Listening to Oars Tower in the Garden of the Couple's Retreat, where one may appreciate the symphony of the lapping pond and the rustling leaves

The Fragrant Isle in the Humble Administrator's Garden, constructed in the shape of a boat. Its various parts represent or even mimic the various parts of a boat. This is a common sort of structure in Chinese gardens.

The Tassel-Washing Pavilion in the Master of Nets Garden. Its name is taken from a line of folklore that dates back to the Spring and Autumn Period (770- 476 BC).

The Lotus Pavilion, surrounded by trees, is the best place in the garden to enjoy breezes on hot, humid days

Across from the yellow rockery, the Mountain Water Loft in the Garden of the Couple's Retreat lies on the water as if it were floating. The scene calls to mind the famous verse, "Drinking not to savor the wine, but rather the landscape."

The Pavilion upon the Water in the Garden of Meditation takes its name from a line of verse that describes the beauty and fragrance of a lotus in autumn. The pavilion spreads its curved eaves over the clear water. Reflections of white clouds and blue sky create a vivid scene.

The Pavilion of Moon and Wind in the Master of Nets Garden has a delicate shape like a bird taking flight. It is particularly attractive covered with snow and ice.

The Pavilion

Pavilions are relatively small structures that serve to embellish the garden. Arranged according to their various shapes and sizes, pavilions come in numerous forms, including square, oblong, hexagonal, octagonal, round, plum-blossom shaped, clover shaped and fan shaped. Their tilting roofs may have either single or double eaves, though single eaves are more common. A pavilion by the water is suitable for appreciating aquatic scenery. One on a mountain is good for appreciating wide vistas. In the Humble Administrator's Garden, there are a total of eighteen pavilions.

The Asking-the-Fountain Pavilion, which faces the rockery, is the best spot in the garden for appreciating mountainous scenery.

The Pavilion in the Lotus Breeze is in the center of the garden. Three of its sides are over the pond. The pavilion is awash in the fragrance of lotus blossoms, carried from afar by a gentle breeze.

The Celestial Spring Pavilion, a double-eave octagonal structure with a gabled roof, has a well inside, which is said to be a Yuan Dynasty (1206- 1368) relic. A pine forest and surrounding green land adds to the atmosphere.

In the Tranquil Residence among Phoenix Trees and Bamboo in the Humble Administrator's Garden, one can experience the unique poetry of the scenery by looking out through the four moon gates.

The Tower Reflection Pavilion is in the center of the pond, in the southeast corner of the western section of the garden. It commands a wonderful view of the water.

The Surging Waves Pavilion lies on top of a rockery in the central part of the garden, surrounded by a natural landscape of age-old, green plants.

The Fry Pavilion in the Garden of Cultivation was built in the Ming Dynasty. There are colorful paintings on its beams. It stands on the side of the pond – one is pulled, as if by magic, to its balustrade to gaze out upon the fish.

Embraced by flowers and plants, the Cold Spring Pavilion in the Master of Nets Garden is quite imposing. Its two eaves are like birds in flight, symbolizing wisdom's pursuit of freedom.

The Pavilion of Genuine Interest was built on the water, with an adjoining shed shaped like a basket of flowers. Its name comes from an inscription by Emperor Qianlong of the Qing Dynasty. Inside the pavilion there are pillars carves with images of phoenixes flying past peonies. Six folding screens are also there, embellished with images of flowers and portraits, and surrounded on three sides by golden lions.

The zigzagging roofed corridor in the Humble Administrator's Garden. The green surroundings lend it a poetic feeling.

By the side of the pond in the Humble Administrator's Garden, a roofed corridor extends under willow trees, linking to the zigzagging bridge leading to the Pavilion in the Lotus Breeze.

Corridors

Corridors link various parts of gardens, connecting buildings, water and rockeries. They not only make it convenient for visitors to travel between different areas of the garden, but also increase the depth of the scenery. There are various styles of corridor, such as open, half-open, double, winding, over water, two-story and sloping. Walking along a zigzagging corridor is like walking on waves.

The double corridor in the Surging Waves Pavilion is an integrated construction, cut off by a wall with fancy windows that disclose a kaleidoscope of scenery.

One side of the double corridor, along which one can appreciate rockery and water scene through the windows

In the Lingering Garden, a roofed corridor off the Hanbi Mountain Villa leading to the Osmanthus Fragrance Pavilion. It climbs up the mountain and enriches the scenery of the garden.

The two-story corridor of the Mountain-in-View Tower in the Humble Administrator's Garden. Water flows under the structure, creating a surreal scene.

Half over the water, this long roofed walkway in the Humble Administrator's Garden makes the visitor feel as if he is walking upon the surface of the water.

This corridor upon water zigzags like graceful waves. Around the corner is a small yard, and rocks by the wall augment the view.

The Small Flying Rainbow is a roofed bridge. It looks out from the north onto the little Canglang, and onto a profound and varying vista. Reflections of the Pavilion of Lotus Breeze and the Fragrant Isle blend into the view, as well as a part of the Mountain Viewing Tower.

A winding corridor above the water in the Humble Administrator's Garden connects to the eastern corridor of the 36 Pairs of Mandarin Ducks Hall. It is surrounded by clear water and has a terrace for fishing, making this environment particularly unique.

A corridor in the courtyard of Enlightenment Hall at the Surging Waves Pavilion

The Leaning-On-Rainbow Bridge in the Humble Administrator's Garden dates back to the Ming Dynasty, displaying its delicacy in the sunshine.

Bridges

Bridges in gardens serve to link the scenic splendors of opposing pond or river banks. They serve not only to enhance aquatic scenery, but also to enrich natural scenery, in combination with the garden's other structures.

Built close to the water's surface, this little flagstone bridge in the Garden of Cultivation is simple and delicate. It dates back to the Ming Dynasty (1368-1644).

The Jiejia Bridge in the Lion Forest Garden sits behind an ancient gingko. Visitors who see it cannot help but think of antiquity.

The zigzag bridge from the Mid-Lake Pavilion in the Lion Forest Garden has a plaque reading "Viewing the Waterfall". This bridge stretches to the shore of the lake and has a strong aesthetic link to the lakeside scenery.

The Leading to Quietude Bridge in the Master of Nets Garden is only two meters long. It looks like a bow or a crescent moon. It is considered one of China's finest stone arch bridges.

Decorations

Decorative objects in Suzhou gardens are generally simple, ingenious and refined. They are masterfully carved and graven. Exterior decorations are things such as windows, bricks window plaques, railings and hangings, while interior decorations are things like woodcarvings, screens and panels. There are two kinds of screen, the above ground wood frame and the standing wood frame.

Part of the standing wood frame in the Mountain Water Loft in the Garden of the Couple's Retreat

In the Mountain Water Loft in the Garden of the Couple's Retreat, this standing wood frame is elaborately engraved with images of plants that symbolize happiness.

The above ground wood frame in the Keep and Listen Pavilion in the Humble Administrator's Garden is made of gingko wood. There are vibrant, engraved images of pine, bamboo and birds. These things represent happiness in life.

The standing wood frame in the Cloud Stairway Hall in the Master of Nets Garden, engraved with images representing good wishes

The furnishings of the Old Hermit Scholar's Hall can be seen on the next two pages. This hall in the Lingering Garden is an outstanding example of a double-sided hall, divided into southern and northern wings by screen doors, carved wooden moon gates and window screens. A plaque reading "Lin Quan" indicates relaxation and retreat; "Qi" refers to high-ranking people; "Shuo" refers to people of outstanding reputation. The whole inscription therefore describes this hall as being a place of rest and retreat for people of high status and luminaries. Six exquisitely designed screen doors sit in the middle of the hall. They are carved of gingko and depict the Cloud-Capped Peak. The carvings on the left and right wooden moon gates are mainly vines, with their branches and leaves protruding. Between the gates are hanging bottle gourds. The window screens are decorated with calligraphy and paintings that match the furniture. The panels in the long window in the northern section of the hall display images of eight Taoist immortals, flowers and characters from famous plays. The southern windows are carved with images of a fisherman, a woodcutter, a farmer and a scholar. The marble screen is an item from a previous owner's personal collection.

Furnishings

Furnishings in Suzhou gardens are designed not only for the needs of daily life, but also to match the architecture of their surroundings. Some extraordinary kinds of furniture include lighting equipment, antiques, calligraphy, paintings and potted landscapes. Furniture, more than anything else, allows us a glimpse into the aesthetic sense of a particular owner of a garden.

Furnishings in grand buildings are quite formally arranged, while those in smaller buildings are arranged more according to a certain style or function.

Suzhou garden furnishings are mainly from the Ming and Qing dynasties. The Ming Dynasty style is simple and grand, with an emphasis on naturalness. The Ming Dynasty furniture is never too flexible, nor too stiff. Keep an eye out for the Ming stools, chairs, desks, tables, teapots, cabinets, couches and folding screens!

A flower holder in the Hall of Swallow's Blessing in the Lion Forest Garden

The 10,000 Volume Hall in the Master of Nets Garden, used as an office and reception room. The couplet on the columns describes a garden scene. The hall's elegant and luxurious furniture is in the Ming style.

The furnishings of the Celestial Hall of the Five Peaks in the Lingering Garden are very precious. Bronze rubbings flank the folding screen.

The upright, wooden framework of the Five Ancient Pines Garden in the Lion Forest Garden. How elegant, with its graceful silk paintings!

The furnishings in the 36 Pairs of Mandarin Ducks Hall in the Humble Administrator's Garden are in an extremely luxurious style. A hanging horizontal banner and a delicate folding screen occupy the center. The overall effect is quite striking.

The wooden desks and stools in the Hall of Distant Fragrance in the Humble Administrator's Garden have elaborate engraved designs.

The furnishings in the boudoir in the Master of Nets Garden are veiled by gauze. There is a dressing table, as well – a rare feminine element.

Moon Gates and Windows

Moon Gates without doors can be found in many buildings throughout the gardens, most often along yards, double corridors and pavilions. Many walls are decorated with mostly unadorned windows. Moon gates provide fresh air and passage; they also provide an interesting frame for scenery.

In the western hall of the Five Ancient Pines Garden, unique ornamental frames with a design of banana trees

A view through a moon gate on one side of the Five Ancient Pines Garden in the Lion Forest Garden

Architectural Objects

The classical gardens of Suzhou cannot be considered complete without a variety of architectural objects like whitewashed walls, moon gates, door and window openings and mosaic walkways. Walls themselves come in many styles such as flat, wave-framed, trapezoidal and perforated. Walls are often visible from other walls, adding a repetitive element to an otherwise chaotic area of the garden. Walkways in Suzhou gardens are also highly esteemed, involving fine mosaic pictures of brick and pottery. These mosaics often have folk themes.

The moon gate in the Humble Administrator's Garden links the middle and western parts. Through it the 36 Pairs of Mandarin Ducks Hall can be seen, right beyond the zigzag corridor.

A peculiar autumn leaf-shaped gate with banana trees and windows, in the Surging Waves Pavilion

Through a gate called "Exploring Tranquility" in the Lion Forest Garden, the Nine Lions Peak rockery can be seen.

Yu Ou Gate and Qinlu Gate in the Garden of Cultivation extend to the tranquil paradise

Haopu Pavilion and the Zigzag Stream Tower in the Lingering Garden, seen through a window

A view from a window in the Zigzag Stream Tower, looking out onto the window openings of the Refreshing Breeze Pavilion by the pond

A window scene in the double corridor of the Lion Forest Garden. The scenery varies from side to side. Round windows certainly add character!

A scene through a window in the Prunus Mume Pavilion in the Master of Nets Garden. The pavilion seems to float on the water.

Window opening design of the Zigzag Stream Tower in the Lingering Garden

Open Window Designs

Open windows embellish garden scenery, dividing yards and linking different landscapes. Take the window openings in the double corridor of the Surging Waves Pavilion for example, how they block certain views and amplify others. A variety of window designs are common, like simple, elegant square ones and curvilinear, imposing round ones.

Window opening in the Master of Nets Garden

Window opening at the Surging Waves Pavilion

Window opening in the Master of Nets Garden

A round window opening in the Garden of the Couple's Retreat, set against flowers

A round window in the Garden of the Couple's Retreat

A chrysanthemum-shaped window in the Surging Waves Pavilion

A window of special design at the Surging Waves Pavilion

A window opening in the Flower Basket Hall of the Lion Forest Garden

An octagonal window in the Daohe Hall of the Master of Nets Garden

A window opening in the Hall of Swallow's Blessing in the Lion Forest Garden

A mosaic walkway with a crane design in the Lingering Garden

A fish design in front of the Mingse Building of the Lingering Garden

A fan-shaped design in the pavement in the Master of Nets Garden. This is quite a meaningful design in Chinese culture.

A mosaic representing five blessings and longevity in the Surging Waves Pavilion

Walkways

Walkways in Suzhou gardens come in various styles and colors. Building interiors are usually paved with square bricks, while corridors often use rectangular slabs. Walkways are always arranged in simple, geometric patterns. Exterior walkways vary in accordance with their surroundings, and may use pebbles and stones. Walkways show off the garden designer's creativity.

A mosaic found in the pavement of the eastern part of the Five Peaks Library. There is a crane in the middle, symbolizing longevity, and five bats around the perimeter that bring happiness and blessings.

A wave wall in the Lingering Garden, obscured by surrounding foliage

Surrounded by water on three sides, the Leaning-on-Rainbow Pavilion in the Humble Administrator's Garden is a classic example of distant view borrowing. The borrowed scene here is the North Temple Pagoda.

Looking through this window, one can see the North Temple Pagoda several miles away.

Borrowed and Contrasting Scenes

Borrowing scenery refers to the integration of large-scale scenery outside the garden, or in a distant area of the garden, into the local garden design. This technique links the garden to its exterior and provides a profound sense of depth. As the great designer Ji Cheng of the Ming Dynasty remarked, borrowing scenery is crucial to garden design. Views that may be borrowed include mountains, rivers, city walls and pagodas. Nearby scenes are also occasionally borrowed, things like buildings and trees.

A contrasting scene at the Good for Both Families Pavilion and a moon gate, as viewed from the Tower of Reflection in the Humble Administrator's Garden

A view of the Tower of Reflection from the Good for Both Families Pavilion, which borrows scenes from the middle part of the garden

A typical example of nearby scene borrowing can be found in the Good for Both Families Pavilion in the western part of the Humble Administrator's Garden. Contrasting scenes use the surrounding landscape to create contrast.

With whom shall I sit? – The scenery of the Fan Pavilion viewed from a moon gate

A view from the west doorway of the Fan Pavilion, looking out onto 36 Pairs of Mandarin Ducks Hall

A view of the Tower of Reflection from the Fan Pavilion's east gate

Through this fan-shaped window opening in the rear of the Fan Pavilion, the Straw Hat Pavilion is clearly visible.

The view behind the Fan Pavilion, through the fan-shaped window

4. Ornamental Plants and Flowers

Plants and flowers are essential in Suzhou gardens. Natural landscapes are certainly more enchanting with willows on riverbanks, pines on mountain peaks, orchids in valleys and lotuses on the water. Plants and flowers, though relatively minor garden elements in terms of design, also serve to embellish rockeries and streams. Certain plants are rich in cultural connotations, and plants are tactfully arranged in the classical gardens of Suzhou to mimic nature. Special care must be taken in their cultivation, as regards geography and ecology. Vines often accompany evergreen trees; flowers accompany bamboo. Ornamental plants go well with their surroundings and add vitality to the garden, enlightening its main themes.

Ivy and wisteria on the stonework in the Master of Nets Garden

Species of Plants and Flowers

In the classical gardens of Suzhou, one can find more than 200 different species of plant. Woody, shade-making trees are prominent, many of which are types of foliage, and some of which are evergreens with ornamental leaves. There are a number of ornamental flowers and fruits decorating the gardens, too. Ivy and other vines can be found by rockeries, walls and flower pergolas. Bamboo is at least as important as pine, in that it remains green and tall through the cold winter. Herbs are grown in yards by windows and at the bases of walls. Aquatic flowers make ponds look more lively.

Green bamboo at the surging Waves Pavilion

Ornamental flowers, like these flowering crabapples, can be seen from the boudoir of the Master of Nets Garden.

Pomegranate in the Garden of Embroidery

Exciting scenes of plum blossoms and other vegetation surround the Snow and Cloud Pavilion. There are also maple trees, willows, bamboo and pine trees.

Magnolias in the Master of Nets Garden attract visitors with their colors and fragrance.

A thorny tree known as the "Perchless" tree

Arrangement of Plants and Flowers

Trees are planted either in an isolated fashion, or clumped together. Isolated trees are scenes in and of themselves. Their delicate shapes can be appreciated from many angles.

Chinese wisteria with curly branches on the pergola on the Small Fairy Isle in the Lingering Garden. How sweet their fragrance!

The branches of this gingko in the Lion Forest Garden add depth to this vista of the Mid-Lake Pavilion and the platform of the Pavilion of Genuine Interest.

Exuberant trees conceal the Mountain Water Loft in the Garden of the Couple's Retreat. It is a mysterious and richly varied site.

A roofed corridor that wraps around the pond neatly divides the Garden of Meditation. The large pond and small buildings make the space seem small. Trees correct for this.

Five or six towering trees embrace the Surging Waves Pavilion. They are set radially around the pavilion, thus forming a symmetrical scene.

The golden leaves of the gingko by the pond in the Lion Forest Garden are rich and fine in autumn.

In the middle part of the Humble Administrator's Garden, one can view different scenery while walking in the shade of trees, along the zigzagging, roofed corridor that leads to the Isle of Fragrance. The bridge and willows form the surrounding scenery, and lotuses and tree branches compose a scene in the moderate distance. Gradually, the Isle of Fragrance becomes a distant vista.

The spectacle of the Abundant Harvest Pavilion, surrounded by its attendant loquats, looks beautiful, especially with its golden early summer fruit.

The trees around the Waiting-for-Frost Pavilion in the middle part of the Humble Administrator's Garden add flavor to the smaller rockeries and buildings.

III – Aesthetic Principles

Suzhou gardens are much more than groups of substantial constructions and scenery. They symbolize the cultural pursuits of their occupants. They demonstrate how their owners pursued the paradox of living in both comfort and luxury. In an effort to retreat from the hubbub of worldly society, the erudite scholars who dwelt in these gardens attempted to return to innocence, that is, to embrace the landscape of nature that these gardens ingeniously mimic, without sacrificing comfort. The beauty of changing scenes! Pavilions, corridors, railed aisles deep in evergreen woods and seas of blossoms, where man is an integral part of nature ... here in these gardens, people found it possible to live in a poetic and comfortable paradise. This was the highest spiritual pursuit, and the ultimate aim of garden construction in Suzhou.

Walking through the gardens, we try not only to appreciate the beauty of the scenic spots with our mere five senses, but also with our sense of history. We try to imagine what the ancients thought as they walked the very same paths; we try to understand their sensibilities and culture. Every detail of the buildings is unique and well designed, including their initial planning, layout, furniture and decorations. Artistic skills were applied not only in construction, but also, perhaps more importantly, in planning, considering geographic features and the like. Themes found throughout the gardens on plaques and couplets on pillars, in furniture, windows, sculptures and mosaics, reflect the traditional poetic and spiritual pursuit. Couplets in halls are good examples. They serve to bring together the glorious Chinese cultural elements of history, poetry and calligraphy. The selection and layout of furniture, the paintings, the designs and colors of the mosaics, the carved stones in the corridors – these are all of paramount artistic value, and of historic and cultural value, as well.

The plants and flowers in Suzhou gardens, those that cluster around buildings and rockeries, remind us of the ancients' cultural intentions. Different plants and flowers have different cultural connotations. Pine stands for pride, plum blossoms and orchids stand for elegance, the lotus indicates purity and nobility, chrysanthemum stands for firm characteristics, peony represents richness and bamboo represents an upright personality. Plants and flowers can be enjoyed all year – willows in spring, crepe myrtles in summer, red maples in autumn and camellias in winter. With such a great variety of plants and flowers, Suzhou gardens truly provide a kaleidoscope of changing scenery. Sometimes there is contrast, but there is always an overall feeling of harmony, the very harmony of nature. Visitors have been enchanted for many generations.

1. Elegance, Grace and Ease

Suzhou gardens are modeled after nature because it was the desire of their owners to return to nature in some substantial way. They are not complete imitations of nature, but are rather stylized in a way that allows them to be believable in such limited space. Architectural art in gardens serves not only to augment the scenery, but also to incorporate Confucian and Taoist elements. Poetic imagery is concealed among the buildings and plants, adding a rich world of literary associations to the garden. Small-sized rockeries, ponds and pavilions really do reflect a profound and splendid cultural spirit. What is shown serves as a reminder of the past and also stimulates the viewer's imagination. The viewer is not separate from the garden; rather, he is part of it, and by extension a part of nature. This does not mean that the viewer is passive. If anything, viewing a Suzhou garden reminds one to live life elegantly and comfortably, unperturbed by stress and corruption. Everything can be seen as a pleasure. This message is what is really unique about Chinese gardens.

The Hall of Erudition and Elegance in the Garden of Cultivation is the garden's main buildings. Its name makes reference to the verse, "being erudtte and elegant, knowing great men from the past." Two hanging couplets lay bare the former owner's intention – one describes a peaceful scene that has witnessed the change of dynasties, the other makes reference to the link between modern and ancient scholarship. These can be considered memorial couplets, and they go perfectly with the garden's enchanting, nostalgic scenery.

The Temple of 500 Sages in the Surging Waves Pavilion, built by Tao Shu, exhibits engravings of famous lines of literature from Suzhou, spanning many different dynasties. They are intended to be an example for later generations.

An inscription, "Records of Rebuilding the Surging Waves Pavilion", on a stone stele, written by Song Qian in the Qing Dynasty

Stone Steles and Tablets

A large number of inscribed stone tablets and steles can be found in the gardens of Suzhou. They are important decorations and symbols of scholarly art. The inscriptions are written in masterful calligraphy. Their content records changes in the gardens.

The Willow by the Surging Waves in the Surging Waves Pavilion

Inlaid on the side of the south corridor of the Surging Waves Pavilion are rubbings of Tao Shu's inscription, In Praise of the Five Seniors. *Tao was the circuit inspector of Jiangsu. The Five Ancient Seniors' names are Pan Yijuan, Han Guiling, Shi Yunyu, Wu Yusong and Tao Shu.*

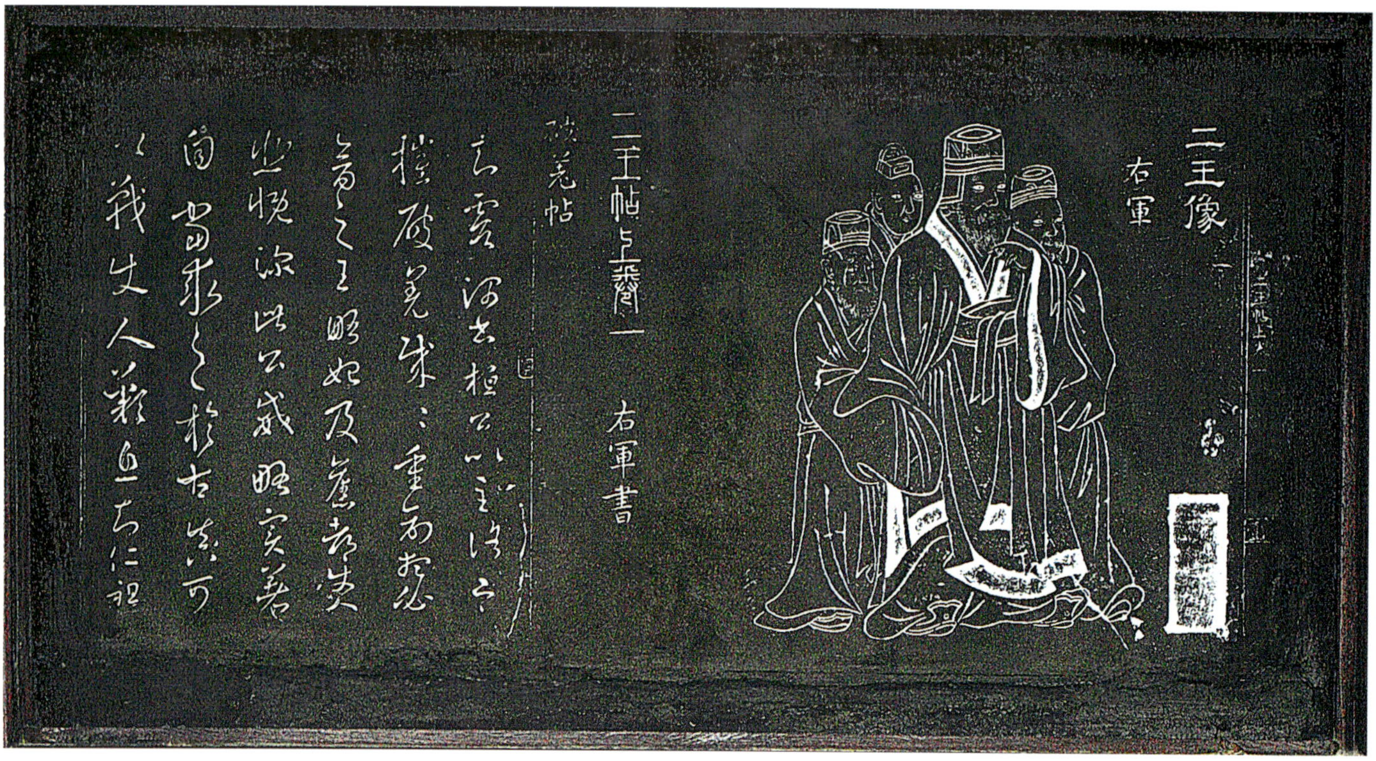

More than 300 stone tablets are preserved in the Lingering Garden, among which calligraphic works by Wang Xizhi and Wang Xianzhi are the most valuable. They are on the wall of a corridor in the Osmanthus Fragrance Pavilion.

This poem, written by Wen Tianxiang in praise of plum blossoms when the Mongolian army imprisoned him, is written in a fine cursive hand. Wen Tianxiang was the prefect of the Pingjiang District of Suzhou in the Southern Song Dynasty (1127- 1279). This poem shows him to be patriotic and upright, and quite intrepid. This picture can be found in the Lion Forest Garden.

Stone steles, mainly inscribed with calligraphic works, are important decorations for buildings. These are steles hanging from the wall of a long roofed corridor in the Lion Forest Garden.

The Room for Worshipping Wen and Shen was built in praise of Ming painters Wen Zhengming and Shen Zhou. In the wall of the room are memorial tablets of stone with line engravings of their portraits, and "A Record of the Wangs' Humble Administrator's Garden" by Wen Zhengming.

Portrait of Wen Zhengming

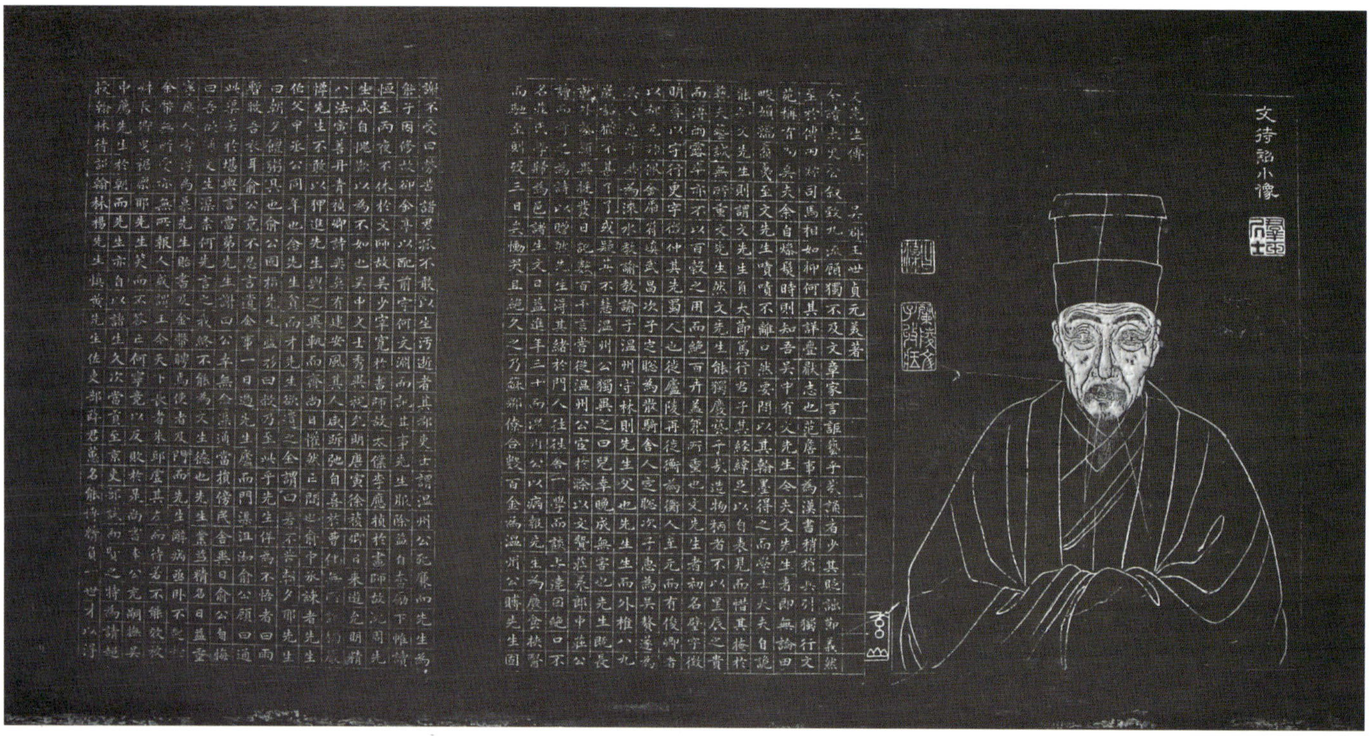

Portrait of Shen Zhou

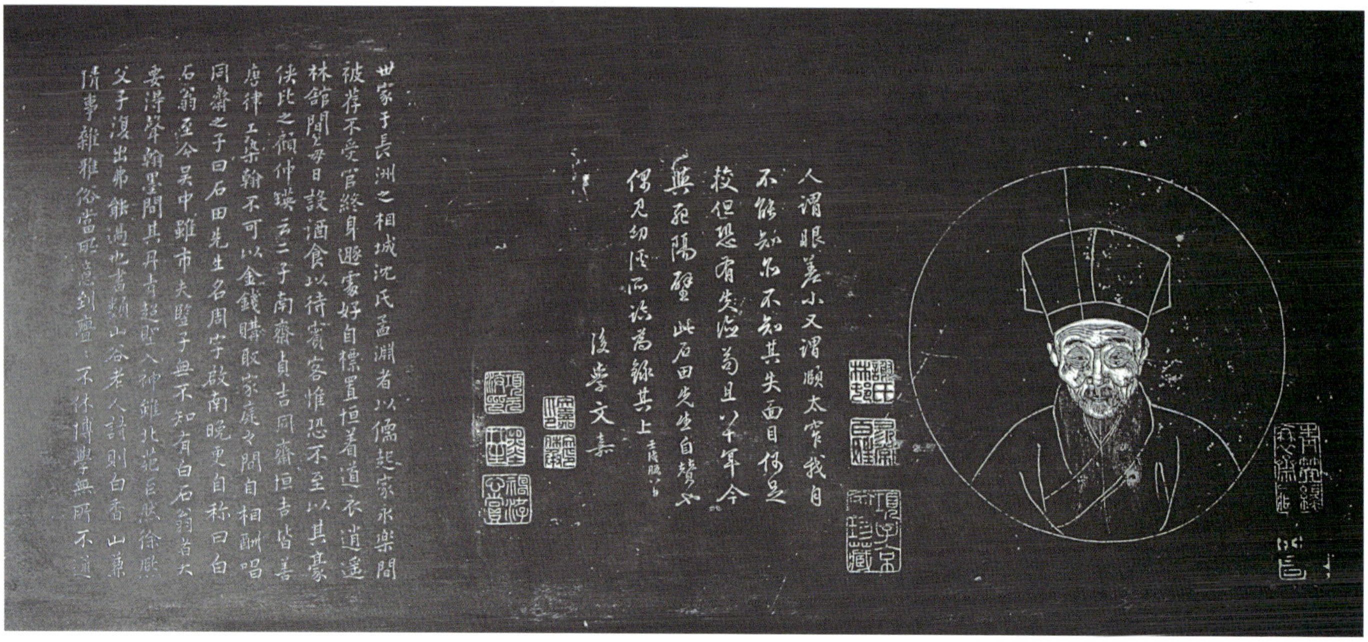

The Small Hall of Ambition in the Humble Administrator's Garden is decorated with various charming stones with lovely shapes. How attractive!

Ornamental Stones

Elegant ornamental stones have a close relationship with Suzhou garden aesthetics. They are always small and delicately shaped. They are often placed on tea tables for decoration, and are considered an expression of the owner's spiritual life.

A spring image of "green hills and verdant plants in the sun"

A summer image of "clouds hidden deep in the mountains"

An autumn image of "dew and mist across the river"

A winter image of "freezing fountain and moon"

Marble wall hangings in the 10,000 Volume Hall in the Master of Nets Garden

Windows

Spring, summer, autumn and winter-themed windows, found in the corner of the zigzag corridor of the Surging Waves Pavilion

Spring – peach blossoms compete for attention

Summer – lotus fragrance, spread by the breeze

Autumn – fruiting pomegranates

Winter – plum blossoms in the snow

A window with a chessboard theme

A window with a string instrument theme

A window with a painting theme

A window with a book theme

Four window openings found on a wall in the back yard of the Nine Lions Peak in the Lion Forest Garden

Wood Carvings

Wood carvings can be found in every garden in Suzhou. They are made to be lofty, simple and elegant. They appear in hinging boards, window frames and furniture. They are a unique sort of embellishment.

A broad window can be divided into five parts: the top, the frame, the middle, the skirt and the bottom. Here, some of the most elaborate wood carvings can be found, for the style often varies from part to part.

The crane-neck pillar on top of the Flower Basket Hall in the Lion Forest Garden is carved into the shape of a wooden flower basket.

These upright wooden windows in the Flower Basket Hall are quite elegant, featuring a combination of simple and complex designs.

A wood carving in the middle part of a hanging board in a hall of the Garden of the Couple's Retreat, designed with three Chinese characters that mean "blessing", "festivity" and "longevity".

A wood carving from a broad window in the Garden of the Couple's Retreat

A wood carving from the standing wood frame of a moon gate in the Garden of the Couple's Retreat. It has a design of fruits that represent good wishes.

Designs on the board of a broad window in a hall of the Humble Administrator's Garden. Each part of the design features a hero from folklore. These heroes are believed to bring happiness.

A gateway structure with a brick carving of the characters "Zao Yao Gao Xiang"

Brick Carvings

Brick carvings are a common decorative element in the architecture of Suzhou. One can find polished carvings on the frames of doors and windows. The most exceptional carvings, however, are certainly those that adorn gates. The gate in the Master of Nets Garden is a wonderful example. It is of the highest level of craftsmanship, and its artistic themes evoke nothing short of man's search for a more harmonious life.

The left pillar carving

The right pillar carving

The brick carving over the door of the 10,000 Volume Hall in the Master of Nets Garden is of high artistic value. Four characters are inscribed onto it reading "Zao Yao Gao Xiang" , which means "literary talent aiming high". On the right pillar of the structure is a carving of a scene from the play Guo Ziyi Celebrating His Birthday. It represents the wish for longevity. On the other pillar is a scene from the play King Zhou Wen's Visit to the Sages, which represents the integration of virtue and wisdom. At the Beauty Within Reach Tower, there is a similar, though less extravagant, carving. It display the four characters "Zhu Song Cheng Mao" , which are intend to praise the character of pine and bamboo. The pillar carvings on the Beauty Within Reach Tower show musical instruments and two fish, symbols that represent the fish for happiness. These brick carving have their roots in traditional culture and folk customs. On a whole, they represent public morality and the search for a better life.

A brick carving that represents happiness and blessings

A brick carving expressing the wish for happiness

The Saints of Happiness, Abundance and Longevity on the Temple Building of the Lion Forest Garden

A dragon-design brick carving on the gateway structure in the Garden of Cultivation, with four characters inscribed in the middle, meaning "staunch and unbiased"

Four carved seal-style characters that together mean "retreat" are carved on the brick door of the Master of Nets Garden. Their meaning is closely tied to the delight of Suzhou gardens in general, which have been popular retreats for scholars and nobles throughout history.

The Small Huabu Structure in the Lingering Garden has an inscription by Qian Daxin of the Qing Dynasty. Age-old vines and upright bamboo surround it, forming an elegant architectural scene.

2. Artistic Inspiration and Furnishings

Rockeries, streams and buildings are the main elements of the gardens of Suzhou, but a garden cannot be considered complete without its furnishings!

Furnishings in classical gardens fall into several different categories, including inscriptions and couplets, furniture proper, sculpture, paintings, carvings, steles and paths. Inscriptions and couplets on wooden plaques and stone steles often represent what the owner thought about nearby scenery. Furniture serves the double purpose of aesthetics and utility. Some of the various kinds of furniture are stools and chairs, desks and tables, teapots, cabinets, couches, folding screens, bookshelves, incense burners, standing mirrors and clocks. There are other small, decorative articles, like china, bronze, jade, stones, plates, boxes and baskets. Wood and brick carvings may also be considered to be decorations, but they have deeper meanings as well, expressing wishes for happiness, blessings and longevity. Paintings and calligraphy are of obvious artistic value, as well as mosaic-work.

Hanging Screens

Hanging screens may be made of granite, stones or other materials. They are hung on the wall or a standing wood frame — sometimes even on the furniture. These items are natural pictures, often assuming the appearance of misty clouds or water, or mountain landscapes.

This hanging screen contains 40 marble stones in various shapes. It can be found in the Worshipping Stone Pavilion of the Lingering Garden. Seven stones below are carved with Tao Yuanming's poetry. The couplets on the columns describe the owner's pursuit of moral integrity and kindness of character.

This standing wooden frame holds an inscription dedicated to a "humble room". It lends a cultural atmosphere to the Celestial Hall of the Five Peaks.

On the rear of the same frame is a carved image of pines and chrysanthemum, representing the moral integrity of a scholar.

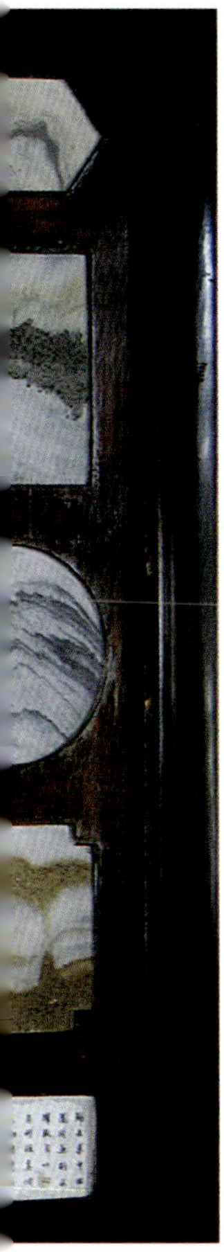

This round, marble slab on a standing wooden frame in the Celestial Hall of the Five Peaks in the Lingering Garden, has a colorful, richly-veined surface which forms a natural landscape, called "Wrapped in Rain and Mist". One can see a bright moon, gentle breezes, mountains and a waterfall. It is a priceless cultural relic.

The Nine Lions Cornerstone is all that remains of an ancient residence built in the Zhizheng period (1341- 1368) of the Yuan Dynasty. It has a carved design of dragons and lions.

The site of the foundation of a "Zen cave", left from the Yuan Dynasty in the Lion Forest Garden

Cultural Relics

Preserved for thousands of years and reconstructed many times, Suzhou's classical gardens still contain many relics of great antiquity. Some steles, for example, while serving important decorative functions, also record the thoughts and ideas of scholars from antiquity, giving our generation important insights into the past.

A peony bed made out of dark stone from the Ming Dynasty. It can be found in the Lingering Garden. More than ten designs are carved onto it, including a motif of two lions playing with a ball.

Light relief on a column base in the Garden of Cultivation

These colorful paintings on the beams of the Fry Pavilion in the Garden of Cultivation date back to the Ming Dynasty. They are of immeasurable value.

Here are two jade carvings in the Prunus Mume Pavilion in the Master of Nets Garden. They were made during the reign of Emperor Qianlong of the Qing Dynasty. Their colors are perhaps even more vivid than when they were made!

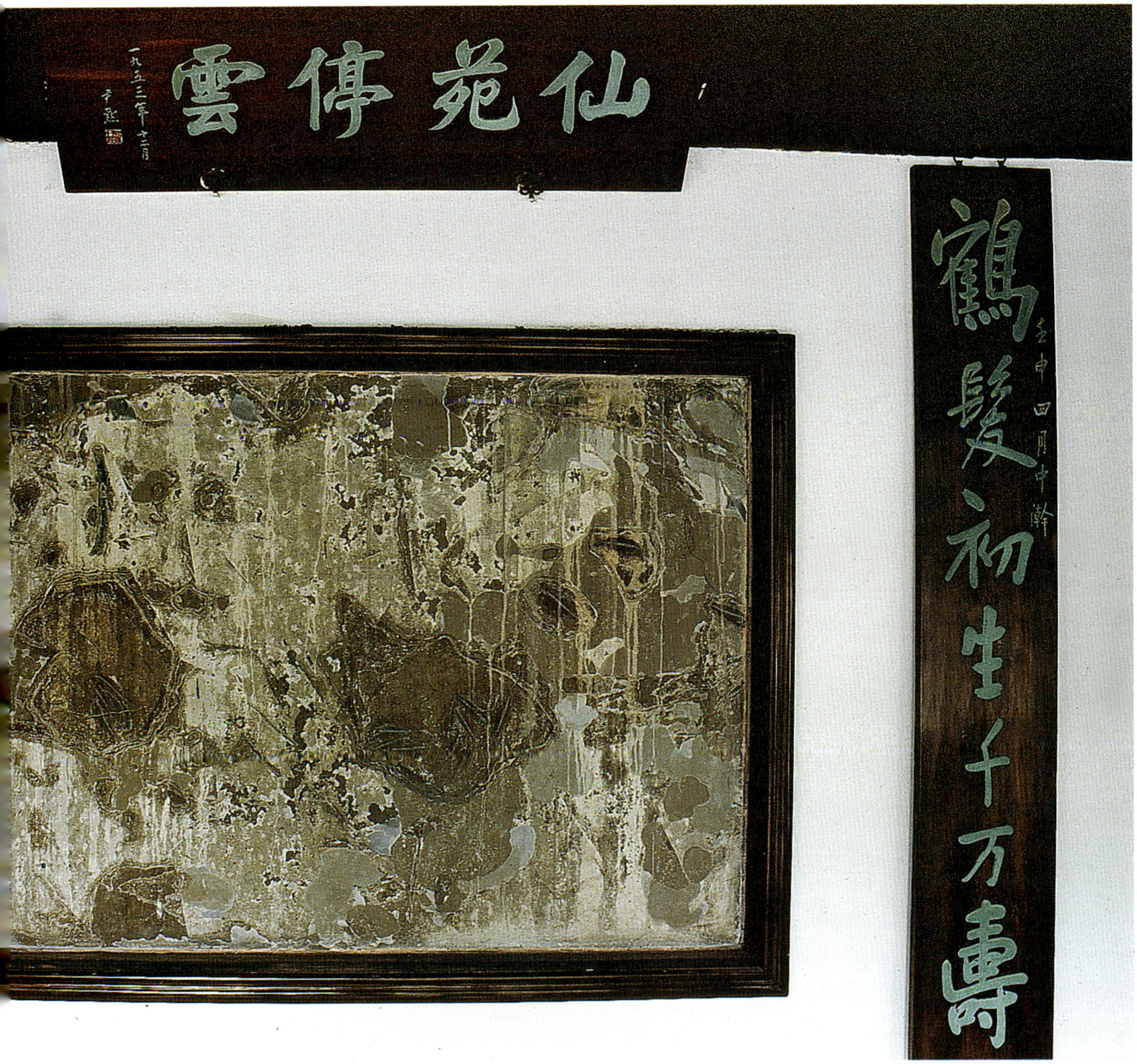

This milky, yellowish fossil in the Cloud-Capped Pavilion is as old as 140 million years. It is 1.65 meters long and 1.3 meters tall. The image of the fish is striking – it looks as if it is swimming happily. The flanking couplets and the inscription on the plaque add to the ambience of the four marble wall hangings. The lake stones, as well as the fossils, strike a delicate harmony with the Cloud-Capped Peak. This expresses the host's desire for longevity.

The inscription on the board banners in the Surging Waves Pavilion is in the handwriting of a famous Qing Dynasty calligrapher.

Inscribed Banners and Couplets

Inscribed banners and couplets are a unique, traditional form in Chinese literary culture. They integrate calligraphy and art with meaningful, poetic content. Famous personages with great taste penned many inscriptions and couplets. They are therefore of great artistic value. The poetic ambience of gardens lies in great part in buildings, inscriptions and couplets.

This couplet quotes two great poets of the North Song Dynasty, Ouyang Xiu and Su Shunqin. The fact that their works are combined into a single couplet speaks to the poets' friendship. It reads, "The gentle breeze and bright moon are priceless, and the landscape is full of affection for man." A borrowed view of Tianping Mountain contributes to the couplet's theme.

This carved brick couplet and the inscription on this plaque describe a harmonious and comfortable daily life for a man and wife. Penned by the former owner, it can be found in the Garden of the Couple's Retreat. The word used for "couple" refers to a Chinese legendary love story about a Cowboy and a Fairy Weaver. This inscription is meant to evoke love and peace.

This couplet, found in the Watching Pines and Appreciating Paintings Studio in the Master of Nets Garden, is written entirely in reduplicated words. It describes early spring, with warblers, swallows, rain and leaves, with the rustling of the wind and a feeling of growing warmth. The words in this couplet take advantage of a linguistic quirk of the Chinese language.

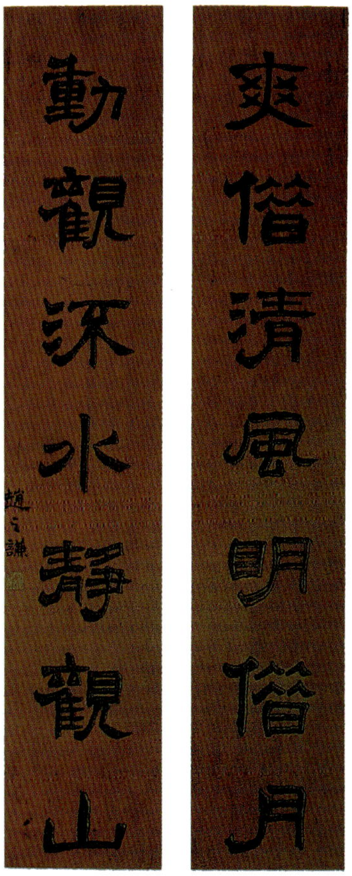

Through the round doors in the walls around the Tranquil Residence Among Phoenix Trees and Bamboo, visitors can enjoy a panoramic, textured view of the central garden. One can also see verdant bamboos and parasol trees. The couplet in the pavilion translates to "The breeze brings coolness and the moon bring light: scenery that moves like water and is as still as a mountain". This poem contrasts motion and stillness, and brightness and darkness.

In the Snow and Cloud Pavilion of the Humble Administrator's Garden, a banner is inscribed with four characters that literally mean "the fragrance of snow, the luxury of clouds". The cursive handwriting of a master calligrapher hangs on the southern eave and pillar. It is a famous couplet that reads, "Cicada sounds add peace to the forest, bird songs add depth to the mountains."

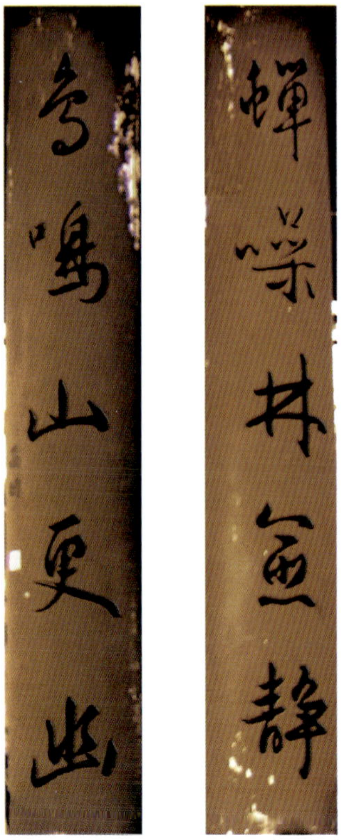

This couplet hanging on the wall of the Tassel-Washing Pavilion in the Master of Nets Garden encourages later generations to learn industry and virtue from their ancestors.

The view from this fan-shaped window in the With-Whom-to-Sit-By Pavilion reminds us of a poem written by Su Shi that expresses a willingness to sit alone under a bright moon in the gentle breeze. A couplet hangs in the pavilion – it is a poem by Du Fu, written in clerical script. It invites a companion to come along to appreciate natural beauty.

The poetic name of the Pavilion of Lotus and Breeze stirs feelings of beauty. The roof is hexagonal and there is water on three sides of the structure, so it commands a radial vista. The couplet on the pillars describes a poetic image, "A pavilion and a pond of lotuses, willows on the bank."

3. Implications of the Artificial Landscape

In the classical gardens of Suzhou, visitors can appreciate grand halls and pavilions, poetry and literature. According to Chinese sentiment, these things cannot be dissevered from the idea of nature; that is, just look out the window, and you will see for yourself how many words a picture is worth.

A lotus pond with chanting frogs, colorful flowers and green foliage, birds flying towards the blue sky, fish swimming happily in the pond, pavilions and stonework – these are all elements of the landscape. A garden needs themes, sounds, colors, vigor and tranquility to be complete. Spring comes when the bamboo shoots up; summer arrives when the pomegranates become red; apricots maturing foretell a golden autumn; and fragrant plum blossoms endure the bitter cold of winter. Plants like peonies, peach trees, crabapples, winding vines and straight pines all bring grand, picturesque Nature down to a manageable scale.

Outside of their natural virtue, all the accoutrements of gardens, artificial gardens and streams, are important in that they display the ideals of their various owners. For instance, plum blossoms, orchids, bamboo and chrysanthemum represent gentlemen; preach blossoms, willows, flowers and grass represent ladies. Natural landscapes of flowers, rocks and streams are almost anthropomorphic (they are certainly good listeners, at least!) In this way, man becomes a natural part of nature.

To the south of the 36 Pairs of Mandarin Ducks Hall is the Hall of 18 Camellias, with pinus bungeana and, of course, camellias.

The Magnolia Hall in the Humble Administrator's Garden is a Ming building with an enclosed court. It is named for the white magnolias in front of the court, which grow sweet in spring.

Affection for Plants and Flowers

Plants and flowers contribute a great deal to the scenery of Suzhou gardens. Small scenic areas in front of and behind halls often have floral themes. Many structures in gardens take their names from plants and flower, referring to the dominant features of the scenes that they command.Take the Humble Administrator's Garden, for instance: its Distant Fragrance Hall is so named because it faces the lotus pond; the Waiting for Frost Pavilion is thus named because of the orange trees by its side that themselves turn orange at first frost; the Tranquil Residence among the Phoenix Trees and Bamboo is named after nearby trees and bamboo; Breeze through the Pines Pavilion is named after the pines; and Magnolia Hall after the magnolia ... such appellations can be seen in every garden. Some ancient trees, in fact, have probably seen all of the changes that have happened to their gardens.

An 800-year-old cypress stands in front of the Watching Pines and Appreciating Paintings Studio, with tangled roots and branches.

The Hall of Distant Fragrance in the Humble Administrator's Garden is situated among the mountains by the water. Lots of blooming lotuses provide scenery for the hall. In summer, lotus blossoms on the lake give off their refreshing fragrance. As Zhou Dunyi described in his essay, the further the fragrance drifts the purer it becomes.

The Keep-and-Listen Pavilion is a nice place for looking out at the rain. The eastern and southern parts of the pavilion both face ponds full of lotuses. The theme of this pavilion is from a Tang poem that reads, "Let's keep the wilted lotus leaves and listen to the rain falling upon them."

The Listening-to-Rain Pavilion in the Humble Administrator's Garden with shady banana trees behind invites visitors to stand and listen to the rain. There are many sound elements used in Suzhou gardens, such as rain, flowing water, and breezes, that combine with other scenery to create an extremely sensual effect.

Golden loquats in the Loquat Garden Court of the Humble Administrator's Garden

The Snow and Cloud Pavilion in the Humble Administrator's Garden is situated on the top of a hill, with water flowing all around. The name of the pavilion refers to snowy white, fragrant plum blossoms and the other plants that surround it. This unique, winter view is perhaps more austere than most.

A famous artist, Wen Zhengming, has a special affection for the Humble Administrator's Garden. When the garden was built and then-owner Wang Xianchen invited him, he was so excited that he planted a creeping wisteria in the yard by the door. Five hundred years later, this wisteria still survives, rugged and splendid (next two pages).

文衡山先生手植藤

Flower Symbols

Owners of Suzhou gardens often used plants to represent their ambitions and thoughts. Different kinds of flowers have different meanings. It is a joy to discover the namesakes of buildings growing in the vicinity, and gazing upon them, feeling them and smelling them.

According to their various features, flowers have over the years been assigned different poetic connotations. Though they make no noise, they still eloquently express their former masters' most profound desires.

Plants and flowers signify elements of character and morality. Pine represents vigorousness, bamboo uprightness, plum blossoms courage, magnolias purity, camellia to brilliance, crepe myrtles to naivete, sweet osmanthus to nobility, peony to prosperity and lotus to elegance.

Plants are an important element of garden design, adding to the ambience of their surroundings. Aside from being arranged according to meaning, plants and flowers are often arranged to mimic how they might occur in nature.

The crab-apple flower symbolizes graceful charm (Lingering Garden).

Magnolias symbolize elegance and purity (Humble Administrator's Garden).

Peonies symbolize richness and prosperity (Lingering Garden).

The lotus represents purity and honor (Humble Administrator's Garden).

Sweet osmanthus stands for prevailing fragrance (Garden of the Couple's Retreat).

Plum blossoms stand for firmness against the elements (Garden of the Couple's Retreat).

Chrysanthemum stands for courage and strength in old age (Lingering Garden).

The Surging Waves Pavilion is the place where many types of bamboo were first cultivated. Over 20 kinds can be seen here, including those with indocalamus leaves, some with green pendulous leaves, Cixiao bamboos and golden bamboos with green purfles. The "delicate green" bamboos are half-covered by banana trees, as described in Su Shunqin's verse. The serenity of bamboo and cypress is a lovely sight (next page).

Pine symbolizes vigor and longevity (Lingering Garden).

Bamboo stands for uprightness (Master of Nets Garden).

Willows stand for charm and loveliness (Lingering Garden).

IV – The Gardens in Perspective

Residences and gardens together are designed, ultimately, for appreciation and habitation. They are spaces for people to read, enjoy music, drink tea, have banquets, watch plays and generally enjoy life. In these gardens, the practical and the aesthetic merge. In this condensed and metaphorical man-made environment, Chinese traditional art and culture prevail and permeate with poetic delicacy. Chinese chess, calligraphy, painting, poetry and tea are all elements of the lifestyle that gardens encourage. Suzhou gardens truly are living representations of Chinese art and culture. The appreciation of the gardens of Suzhou helps us not only to understand Chinese culture, but also to temper our characters.

Our time is one where questions of the coexistence of man and nature are more important than ever before. Perhaps we might look to how these gardens integrate natural scenery with the artificial for some answers to these questions. In them, human beings, the natural world, society and the Tao all live in harmony. They therefore represent the harmony inherent in natural ecosystems. Today we are beginning to bring the legacy of classical gardens into our daily lives. We even go further and attempt to integrate the principles of garden construction into modern projects. For example, the designs of new green spaces, housing developments and even whole cities are beginning to look to the gardens of Suzhou for inspiration.

In ancient times, the experience and ideas accumulated through the construction of gardens in Suzhou made a great impact on Asian and European architectural cultures. They are the basis of the Chinese style. Nowadays, the gardens of Suzhou receive more acclaim than ever. Since 1980, when the Astor Chinese Garden Court was built in the New York Metropolitan Museum of Art, modeled after the Peony Studio in the Master of Nets Garden, a lot of Yangtze delta-style gardens have been constructed all over the world, including the Dr. Sun Yat-Sen Classical Chinese Garden in Vancouver, Canada and the Yun Xiu Yuan Garden in Singapore. Buildings modeled after those found in the gardens of Suzhou are slated to be constructed at UNESCO headquarters in Paris, to serve as yet another platform to share this unique art form. All this shows that the gardens of Suzhou are great ambassadors of Chinese culture. Surely, the gardens of Suzhou are an important contribution to the goal of humans all over the world living in harmony with nature.

1. The Cultural Value of Garden Parks

Suzhou classical gardens vividly epitomize traditional Chinese culture. Indeed, these fascinating gardens have helped us to understand the essence of art and also to improve our characters and temperaments. Their impact on modern culture is not to be underestimated. New parks, residential quarters and city planning all draw upon classical gardens for inspiration. Living happily in perfect balance and harmony with nature is nothing less than the ultimate pursuit of humankind.

The most well-known state scenic areas in Suzhou are in Mudu, Shihu (Stone Lake), Guangfu, Dongshan, Xishan, Luzhi, Tongli and Yushan. There are also provincial scenic areas, such as Huqiu (Tiger Hill) and Fengqiao (Maple Bridge).

Tianping Mountain, located about 18 kilometers from the western border of the city, obtained its name (literally, "sky-smooth") because of its flat top. It is also known to some people as Fan Tomb Mountain because in the mountain are the graves of the ancestors of Fan Zhongyan, a great writer and reformer of the Northern Song Dynasty (960- 1127). The rocks in the mountain have grotesque shapes, and there are constructions among the verdant plants there, among the flaming maple leaves. Naturally beautiful and historically significant, it brings history to life for tourists. A Royal Inscription Pavilion was erected there upon the occasion of a visit from Emperor Qianlong, who left an inscription on a stone among the maples.

劍池

Tiger Hill is the most famous scenic area in Suzhou. As recorded in the history of the Spring and Autumn Period (770- 476 BC), the King of Wu once had his royal palace garden here, and his son Fuchai was buried here. Throughout Chinese history, many emperors and historic figures visited and stayed in this area, including Qinshihuang, the man who unified China, and Sun Quan, one of the three Great Lords of the Three Kingdoms Period (220- 280). In the East Jin Dynasty (317- 420), a great Buddhist temple was built here, which went on to become the most famous temple in the Yangtze delta. Later this spot came to be admired for its scenery. Bai Juyi (772- 846), a Tang poet, regarded it highly, as well as Emperor Kangxi of the Qing. Su Dongpo (1037- 1101), a famous poet, once remarked, "It is a loss to visit Suzhou without seeing Tiger Hill."

Today's attention to the reconstruction of Suzhou's scenic areas is bringing perhaps more tourists than ever before.

A distant view of Fengqiao (Maple Bridge)

Han Shan Temple is located in the Maple Bridge Scenic Area on the western outskirt of Suzhou. It was first established under the reign of Tian Jian (502- 519) of the Liang Dynasty. Its original name was Miao Li Pu Ming Tower Court, which means "Temple of Auspiciousness and Brightness".

During the Zhenguan reign (627- 650) of the Tang Dynasty, Han Shan and Shi De, two famous monks, lived here, which is why the temple is now known as Han Shan. Later, in the first year of the Taiping Xingguo period (976) of the Northern Song Dynasty, a seven-story tower was erected here and the name was changed to Pu Ming Chan Yuan, which means "Prevailing Brightness Zen Court". But from the end of the Yuan Dynasty, through the Ming and Qing dynasties, various structures here were destroyed and rebuilt. Finally, towards the end of the Qing, Fengqiao was restored to its original glory. Many Japanese cherries were then planted there to serve as testimony to China and Japan's friendship.

Han Shan Temple is famous in large part because of a Tang Dynasty poem by Zhang Ji, entitled "A Night Mooring at Maple Bridge".

About five kilometers from the Xumen Gate of Suzhou city, to the southwest, lies Stone Lake. It is a lagoon off of Lake Tai. The legend goes that it was a huge expanse of water at the time that the states of Wu and Yue were at war. The army of Yue, so it is said, tried to cut a canal through a nearby mountain. This is the origin of the lake's name.

Fan Chengda (1126- 1193), a great poet of the Southern Song Dynasty, lived a secluded life here. He built the Stone Lake Cottage. On the north end of a lake lies an ancient bridge called Xingchun (Moving Spring) Bridge, a stone bridge with nine arches. This bridge commands a wonderful view of the surrounding landscape.

It is a custom to visit Xingchun Bridge to watch the moon on the 18th day of the 8th lunar month. According to Fan Chengda, "Those who visit Suzhou without crossing Xingchun Bridge have visited in vain."

Suzhou's numerous canals weave throughout the city. All the water in the city is somehow linked. Bridges not only facilitate transportation, but also contribute to the beauty of the city. This bridge was originally built during the Song Dynasty.

A scene of houses and bridges linked by waterways

The City Planning Exhibition Center by the ancient moat

Renmin Bridge, a modern corridor bridge across the moat

Archaic style constructions on Moye Road along the moat

The Lion Forest residential quarter on Pingjiang River

The Yi Jing Building (a building for Buddhist translations) in Jing Yuan Garden

Jing Yuan (Quietness) Garden is located in the northern part of the Tiger Hill scenic area. The layout of the garden strictly follows the precepts of "arrangement appropriate to land features, well-proportioned designs and scenes as garden features". Borrowed scenes are used here and there. With the contrasting relationships between the various towers, pavilions and corridors, the constructions in the garden look quite refined and attractive. The plants in the garden, indigenous to southeast China, change colors along with the seasons. Tourists staying in this garden may forget even the passage of time.

Jing Yuan Garden set against the distant Tiger Hill Tower

The inscription for Cheng Huai Tower in Jing Yuan Garden

Jing Yuan Garden in seasonal colors

A pavilion upon water in Jing Yuan Garden; a landscape of hills and water

To the west of Suzhou city and by the Taihu Lake lies the famous ancient town Mudu, where the Yans' Garden is situated by the Wangjia Bridge on Shantang Street. Its front gate faces Xiangxi Stream and its rear lies against Lingyan Mountain. This garden used to be the residence of Yan Jiagan from Taiwan. The main hall structured with Phoebe zhennan wood, a construction of the Ming Dynasty looks spacious and grand, rarely seen in the Yangtze Delta area. The so-called "Mini Garden of All Seasons", the major part of it has a well planned layout, which features on appropriate proportion of the closeness of the scenic spots, their relative heights, elegant detailed designs and depths. Because of its unique workmanship in construction, it is justly acclaimed as "the classic Garden of the Yangtze Delta".

Another classic garden in Mudu is Hongying Mountain House, also a famous one of the time of Qianlong Emperor's six visit, for it used to be a place the emperor would visit each time when he came. Here he would get on board a boat and appreciate the operas. The famous ministers of the time such as Liu Yong would also stay here for the nights. The garden consists of two mini gardens, respectively called Xiuye Garden and Xiaoyin Garden.

Besides, there is also a third famous classic garden situated in the same street to the east of Lufei Bridge. It acquired its name for a 500-year-old pine tree. Used in the later period of Qing as a residence of a rich businessman named Cai Shaoyu, it features compactness in layout. Presently it is still kept intact, especially the brick-carved gateway structure, on which is inscribed vivid pictures including a Pipa music instrument. The Phoenix Tower was constructed earlier than the famous carved building at Dongshan town but bears much resemblance to it. Here the visitors can command a good view of the nearby pine tree and the distant Lingyan Mountain.

Lianhua Zhuang (Lotus Village) Park in Huzhou was rebuilt and expanded in March 1987. The architecture in the park, its layout and form, makes full use of the extensive water and land. The buildings are faithfully built in Song and Qing styles, and they manage to add extensive value to the surrounding natural scenery.

Square Tower Park lies in the ancient town of Changshu. Rebuilt in a classical style with its square tower as its centerpiece, this garden replicates the architectural style of the Song Dynasty. It has a lake surrounded by corridors and halls.

2. Garden Parks as a Bridge to the World

Suzhou gardens have become a means of cultural communication. They serve to carry traditional Chinese culture to the world. They provide a wonderful way to communicate and exchange art and culture with other nations.

The Ming Studio, completed in April 1980 in New York's Metropolitan Museum of Art, created a precedent for the exportation of Suzhou's classical garden art. Taking the Peony Studio in the Master of Nets Garden as its basis, the architectural structure and decorations of the Ming Studio are faithful to Ming styles.

The New York Chinese Scholar's Garden, inside the Staten Island Botanical Garden, was finished in February 1998. It covers an area of only 2,500 square meters. However, the garden manages to provide several scenic spots, reproducing spatial elements of the gardens of Suzhou.

The Dr. Sun Yat-Sen Classical Chinese Garden was built in April 1986 in the middle of Vancouver's bustling Chinatown. One hundred thousand Chinese-Canadians sponsored the project. It is named after the founder of the first Chinese Republic, Sun Yat-Sen.

Yun Xiu Yuan (Garden of Beauty), built in 1992, is a special garden within a garden. It is in Yurong Park, in Singapore. It is elegant and largely unadorned. It is the only Suzhou-style landscape garden in Southeast Asia.

Foreign friends striding excitedly over the Leading to Quietude Bridge, the smallest bridge in the Master of Nets Garden

International friends sing the praises of the gardens of Suzhou

Watching a traditional opera in a garden hall

Postscript

It is spring now, the time of blooming and new ventures. What a perfect time to put this exquisite book into print. After profoundly deliberating over its form and content, it finally materializes thanks to the industry of experts, scholars and garden workers. We are led to this landscape of aesthetics, history and culture. The pictures selected for this peerless book have sensually and emotionally captured the gardens' essence. The photographers must love the gardens of Suzhou very much. We look forward to feedback and suggestions from readers.

We extend our heartfelt thanks to the following organizations: Soochow University, University of Science and Technology of Suzhou, Suzhou Foreign Publicity Division of the Municipal CPC Committee, Suzhou Institute of Landscape Architectural Design, Suzhou Landscape Administration, the administrations of the Humble Administrator's Garden, the Lingering Garden, the Master of Nets Garden, the Mountain Villa with Embracing Beauty, the Surging Waves Pavilion, the Lion Forest Garden, the Garden of Cultivation, the Garden of the Couple's Retreat, the Garden of Meditation, the Garden of Harmony, the Listening-to-the-Maples Garden, the Garden of the Five Peaks, the Half Garden, Quyuan Garden, Jing Yuan Garden, the Garden of Embroidery, Hui Yin Garden, Mudu Tour Development industry company, Tiger Hill Scenic Spot, Tian Ping Mountain Scenic Spot, Fengqiao Scenic Spot and Stone Lake Scenic Spot.

The Editorial Committee of
World Heritage Sites in China: The Classical Gardens of Suzhou
Spring, 2007

新世界出版社社长：杨雨前
中国对外翻译出版公司总经理：吴希曾

图书在版编目(CIP)数据

苏州古典园林=The Classical Gardens of Suzhou:
英文/冯朝雄，范贻光主编；杜争鸣，（美）篮雅安
(Lanphier,A.)译.—北京：新世界出版社：中国对外
翻译出版公司，2007.12
(世界遗产•中国)
ISBN 978-7-80228-508-8

Ⅰ.苏… Ⅱ.①冯…②范…③杜…④篮… Ⅲ.古典园林—
简介—苏州市—英文 Ⅳ.K928.73

中国版本图书馆CIP数据核字（2007）第159322号

总编审 Editors-in-Chief
张高里 Zhang Gaoli　张海鸥 Zhang Hai'ou
主任编审 Executive Editors
罗平峰 Luo Pingfeng　岑红 Cen Hong
责任编辑 Editors
罗平峰 Luo Pingfeng　臧惠娟 Zang Huijuan
英文审定 English Revisors
左英 Zuo Ying　张民捷 Zhang Minjie
英文翻译 English Translators
杜争鸣 Du Zhengming　篮雅安 Adam Lanphier
左英 Zuo Ying

出版发行：新世界出版社
社　址：北京市西城区百万庄大街24号（100037）
网　址：www.nwp.cn(中文)
www.newworld-press.com(英文)
邮购电话：+86 10 68998733

出版发行：中国对外翻译出版公司
社　址：北京市西城区车公庄大街甲4号物华大厦六层
网　址：www.ctpc.com.cn
邮购电话：+86 10 68359376 68359303 68359101 68357937

经　销：新华书店
印　刷：苏州工业园区美柯乐制版印务有限责任公司
开　本：889 x 1194 1/16
印　张：12.75
版　次：2008年1月第1版
印　次：2008年1月第1次印刷
定　价：108.00元
标准书号：ISBN 978-7-80228-508-8